# ABOUT Seb Malik

Seb has worked in investment banking for a decade as a risk analyst, derivatives trader (on his personal account) and latterly a BA and PM in a career that has spanned both London and Zurich.

He currently provides MiFID II remediation solutions for investment firms as well as intensive weekend training courses to the public through revivalfinreg.com

He writes regularly on MiFID II and his articles can be found here: www.revivalfinreg.com/articles/

Seb suffers from intractable wanderlust. He is widely travelled having resided in Switzerland, Syria and Egypt. He speaks five languages and is keen to acquire Italian, Spanish and Farsi.

Outside of finance, his passion is writing and his first novel is to be published shortly under his *nom de plume*. He is currently in the throes of writing a thriller. He loves discussing and exchanging ideas; connect with him on LinkedIn and **please consider leaving a review on Amazon**.

D1471869

# MIFIDII

## A Survival Guide

## Seb Malik

Revival Media

MIFIDII: A Survival Guide
ISBN: 9780993546532

First published in Great Britain in 2016 by Revival Media
Copyright © 2016 Seb Malik

**\*\*DISCLAIMER\*\***

Revival Media is a trading name of Revival Media ltd, Kemp House, 160 City
Road, London EC1V 2NX
www.revivalm.com

A CIP catalogue record for this book
is available from the British Library

To my firstborn son.
Forever love.

*En mon païs suis en terre lointaine;*
*Je m'esjouys et n'ay plaisir aucun;*
*Puissant je suis sans force et sans povoir,*
*Bien recueilly, débouté de chascun.*

François Villon

# Contents

*Firms will need to start planning for the MiFID II changes ahead of the finalisation of the EU implementing legislation and the subsequent changes that we and the PRA make to our Handbooks, and changes that HM Treasury makes to financial services legislation.*

*MiFID II is a wide-ranging piece of legislation and, depending on your business model, could affect a wide range of your firm's functions – from trading, transaction reporting and client services to IT and HR systems.*

FCA

# Introduction

Business analysts (BAs) and project managers (PMs) working on MIFIDII will be the main to benefit from this guide. Most tracts I have encountered are either too high level to be of any practical aid, or too detailed (aimed principally at the legal community) leaving the reader overwhelmed.

That the changes required for MIFIDII are not communicated in a single unified document is where this guide earns its keep. The two Level I texts have given birth to a plethora of directives, regulations, 33 Technical Specifications, 11 Implementing Technical Specifications and Level III explanatory texts. These documents total nearly 300 documents. These must be read, digested, cross-referenced, organised and categorised in order to arrive at actionable issues. This one-stop guide is an attempt to do so.

Most of the more detailed Level II texts have now been adopted by the Commission (and passed by the EU Parliament). Project work should be well under way by now. Indeed, regulated markets are already announcing solutions that are designed to circumvent core MIFIDII objectives such as pre-trade transparency (refer to Equity on Trading Venue section). Attention now focuses on Level III interpretative Q&As and guidance especially from ESMA and national regulators, the latter who are in the throes of transposing the directives into national law.

The post financial crash has brought in a slew of regulatory reform aimed at reducing systemic risk, and increasing investor protection. The 2009 G20 summit in Pittsburgh resolved to tackle 'excessive risk-taking [and] to improve the over-the-counter derivatives market'. In this regard the G20 resolved that, '[a]ll standardized OTC derivative contracts should be traded on exchanges or electronic trading platforms, where appropriate, and cleared through central counterparties [and]...should be reported to trade repositories.' EMIR is the EU's regulatory manifestation of this resolution.

This has coincided with existing regulatory change. Investment firms and financial companies have had to grapple with Dodd-Frank, Basel III, EMIR, and MIFID I. PRIIPS (packaged retail and insurance-based investment product); MAD I, II and MAR (Market Abuse Directive/Regulation); Anti-Money Laundering Directive; Senior Managers' Regime and MIFIDII are all going live by 2018.

With this backdrop, BA and PM work is dominated by regulatory change projects. Those with expertise in legislation will be richly rewarded whereas those with generic BA and PM skills will struggle to stay afloat.

I am excited by MIFIDII. It is not without criticism, but I salute the bodies of the European Union for having the courage to enact such a bold suite of legislation. I believe that five years after the go-live date, investors and honest participants will look back with a favourable view. Specifically, it will prevent European markets going down the disastrous US route of market fragmentation with all the

2

concomitant dysfunctionality. There are currently 128 different fixed income trading platforms.[1]

If MIFIDII is enforced then investors will be the winners. High Frequency trading abuse will be tamed, thereby driving orders back into lit markets where currently they are routed to opaque dark pools (with the consequential propensity for market abuse and exploitation of investors). This is to be welcomed.

In order to achieve its noble aims, there is an overhead to be paid (estimated at €2.5bn).[2] For investment firms, this includes extensive IT system changes; new reports; compliance roles and fresh procedures. Upon understanding the legislation, firms should be conducting **impact analyses**, followed by **gap analyses**. Solutions should be **designed** and presented to the project board for approval upon which **functional requirements**, **build**, **testing** and **deployment** should occur. Business analysts and project managers need to be flexible as the FCA is still in the third round of consultation. Subprojects should consider agile techniques to allow for iterative benefits and change.

## How to use this guide

I have bucketed MIFIDII rules into headings: Trade Transparency, Transaction Reporting & Market Data; Trading & Execution; Algorithmic Trading; Investor Protection; Investment Advice; Research; Product Governance and Commodity Derivatives. Where to bucket a particular rule is, of course, subjective and there is overlap.

It is impossible to commit to memory thousands of pages of technical details. What is important is to have a thorough working knowledge of the various aspects of the legislation and to know where to look when detail is required.

With this in mind, I have extensively referenced statements, the majority of which are directly lifted from the source texts with minimal editing. Key words have been marked bold. I anticipate the reader will dip into the minutiae by accessing the relevant sections of the source legislation by clicking on the references links. I have also collated links to all the Key Texts in the Resources chapter. **I strongly advise downloading these principle texts *prior* to commencing this text and having them readily accessible as you read**.

****

Finally, please do connect with me, whether that be to highlight an error, suggest an enhancement or just to say *hi*. I anticipate emailing out minor updates periodically.

I trust this guide will be of use!


Seb Malik
November 2016

# 1
# What is MIFIDII?

MiFIDII: **M**arkets **i**n **F**inancial **I**nstruments **D**irective **II**.
MiFIR: **M**arkets **i**n **F**inancial **I**nstruments **R**egulation.

What in common parlance is referred to as MIFIDII is, in fact, actually both the **directive** and the **regulation** (and associated technical specifications and delegated directives and regulations). ESMA is not empowered to legislate, therefore ESMA technical specification documents should not be referred to directly, rather the Commission's subsequent delegated acts (if accepted and passed by the EU Parliament and Council) carry legal force.

MiFIR and MIFIDII aim to enhance the efficiency, resilience and integrity of financial markets. It is a significant overhaul of the status quo and an attempt to lay down the European Union's regulatory framework from afresh. It will require significant changes to existing systems and processes as well as the introduction of new ones. There will be a significant increase in reporting requirements.

## Benefits

Increased market integration, **efficient** and **transparent** financial **markets**, enhanced **competition** and availability of services or increased **investor protection**. The suggested measures should make financial markets more **transparent** and more secure and **improve investor confidence** and **participation** in financial markets. In addition, by contributing to **reducing markets' disorder** and **systemic risks**, these options should improve the stability and reliability of financial markets.

A **single** set of rules across the entire EU for all institutions will also **avoid** potential **regulatory arbitrage** as well as enhance legal certainty and decrease regulatory complexity for market participants.[3]

## MiFIR Vs MIFIDII

MiFIR is a *regulation* (No 600/2014) which all EU member states must implement in full, as is. There is no discretion or need for transposition into national legislation. In the EU's words: A 'regulation' is a binding legislative act. It must be applied in its entirety across the EU.[4]

MIFIDII is a *directive* (2014/65). A directive is a legislative act that sets out a goal that all EU countries must achieve.[5] However, it is up to the individual countries to transpose by interpreting the directive and then enacting their own domestic laws in order to realise these goals. (This means there will be minor differences between individual member states.)

In the UK, the FCA is the 'national competent authority' that is leading this transposition. The FCA's dedicated MIFIDII page contains detailed discussion on their interpretation of

MIFIDII and how UK firms will be affected. The website is listed in Chapter 13.

## Why the need for MIFIDII?

The existing regulatory landscape has been shaped by various overlapping pieces of legislation. Principle amongst these are Regulation (EU) No 648/2012 on OTC derivatives, central counterparties and trade repositories (**EMIR**) and Markets in Financial Instruments Directive 2004/39/EC (**MIFID I)**.

EMIR, with its overarching objective of reducing systemic risk, lay down mandatory central clearing and reporting requirements for certain classes of OTC derivative contracts (in EMIR's parlance: subject to the *clearing obligation*) and established uniform requirements for the performance of activities of central counterparties and trade repositories. There is considerable overlap with EMIR's *clearing obligation* and MIFIDII's *trading obligation* which mandates obligatory trading on regulated venues for specified classes of derivative contracts.

MIFID I entered into force in 2007. The principle aspects it covered were: Business Conduct: (best execution, client categorisation, suitability, inducements, investment advice, commodity derivatives, reporting requirements, client order handling, marketing and transaction reporting). Organisation (licensing, cross-border passporting [a contentious issue in the post-brexit world], compliance arrangements, risk management, outsourcing, record-keeping, client assets and client money, conflicts of interest, systems and controls, auditors, controllers and governance) and Equity transparency (systemic internalisation, pre-trade transparency and post-trade transparency).

While it contributed to more competition and transparency, the unintended consequence was market fragmentation and an increase in market data costs for investment firms who had to source data from a plethora of lit and dark liquidity sources. The Chief Executive of BATS Chi-X Europe said, '[t]he biggest criticism of MIFID was the fragmentation it brought, but we never received the antidote – the consolidated tape.'[6] MIFIDII now provides this antidote. This near real-time consolidated tape of all trades executed across the EU will allow a one-stop snapshot of the bloc's executions and liquidity a la US consolidated tape (called the **S**ecurity **I**nformation **P**rocessor - SIP).

The consolidated tape *alone* will not prove to be a panacea, just as the SIP has failed to stem market abuse in the US, but that would be to pre-empt the discussion.

MIFID (I) needs to be recast in order to appropriately reflect developments in financial markets, address weaknesses and close loopholes that were exposed in the financial market crisis.[7]

Since then we have had a financial crisis, and a proliferation of:

- novel complex derivative instruments,
- new investors,
- off-exchange private liquidity providers and dark pools leading to a fragmented market,

- high frequency trading firms.

The financial crisis and subsequent market developments made clear that the scope of the Directive was no longer appropriate and that investor protection had to be strengthened further. As mentioned, one of the unintended consequences of MiFID I was the explosion in OTC trading, off-exchange products and lightly or unregulated so-called 'dark' pools which threatened the integrity of the very market thereby increasing systemic risk. MIFIDII seeks to bring all OTC trading onto lit exchanges or organised venues 'and that all such venues are appropriately regulated'.[8]

So, on 15 May 2014 the European Parliament passed:

1. Regulation No 600/2014 (MiFIR): 'The legislation consists of two different legal instruments, a **Directive** and this **Regulation**…This Regulation should therefore be read together with the Directive.' and

2. Directive 2014/65 (MIFIDII).

- Achieving **greater transparency** through the introduction of a **pre and post trade transparency** regime for **non-equities** and strengthening and broadening of the existing equities trade transparency regime;

- Bringing **OTC** trading **onto regulated venues** by the creation of a **new category** of platform **called** the **Organised Trading Facilities (OTF)**. This will capture and regulate trades and orders for 'bonds, structured finance products, emissions allowances and derivatives'[9]

  - and of a trading obligation for shares on regulated venues ; 'Financial counterparties...and non-financial counterparties...shall conclude transactions...in derivatives only on: (a) RMs; (b) MTFs; (c) OTFs; or third-country.'[10]

- **Regulating High Frequency Algorithmic trading** thereby promoting orderly markets.

- Introduction of **position limits** and **reporting requirements** for **commodity derivatives** [thereby reducing systemic risk].

- Broadening the definition of investment firm to capture firms trading **commodity derivatives** as a financial activity

- Strengthening the protection of investors through the enhancement of the **rules on inducements**, a ban on inducements for independent advice and new **product governance** rules

- Introducing provisions on **non-discriminatory access** to trading and post-trading **services** in trading of financial instruments notably for exchange-traded derivatives.[11]

## Definitions

The following acronyms recur frequently; the reader is encouraged to familiarise himself with them. For further definitions, refer to Article 4(1) of (MIFIDII, 2014) which is dedicated to definitions.

**Approved Publication Arrangement (APA)** - a person authorised under [MIFIDII] to provide the service of publishing trade reports on behalf of investment firms pursuant to Articles 20 and 21 of [MIFIR].[12]

**Approved Reporting Mechanism (ARM) -** an authorised person to provide the service of reporting details of **transactions** [on a T+1 basis] to competent authorities or to ESMA on behalf of INVFs.[13]

For further details, refer to the FCA's dedicated ARM page[14].

Below is a list of UK ARMs:

| Organisation | System | ISIN | OTC | AII |
|---|---|---|---|---|
| Euroclear UK & Ireland (EUI) | CREST | Approved (Restricted) | | |
| TRAX | TRAX | Approved | Approved | Approved |
| London Stock Exchange | UNAVISTA | Approved | Approved | Approved |
| Getco Europe Limited | GETCO | Approved | Approved | Approved |
| Abide Financial Limited | TransacPort | Approved | Approved | Approved |
| Bloomberg Finance L.P. | Bloomberg TOMS | Approved | Approved | |

**Consolidated Tape Provider (CTP)** - an authorised person (under MIFIDII) to provide the service of collecting trade reports for financial instruments from RMs, MTFs, OTFs and APAs and consolidating them into a continuous electronic live data stream providing price and volume data per financial instrument;[15] [similar to the US SIP.[16]] Note the differing implementation timescales between equities and non-equities.

**Central counterparty (CCP)** - a legal person that interposes itself between the parties to the contracts traded on one or more financial markets, becoming the buyer to every seller and the seller to every buyer[17].

**Competent Authority** - the authority designated by each Member State [e.g. for the UK, the FCA]

**Financial Instruments -** exhaustively defined in Section C of (MIFIDII, 2014), further elaborated in Articles 4-8, 10, 11 in (Del. Regulation 25.4.2016, 2016)

**INVF** [my, non-MIFIDII, acronym: **INVF**] - any legal person whose regular occupation or business is the provision of one or more investment services to third parties and/or the performance of one or more investment activities on a professional basis.[18]

**Management Body -** The body or bodies of an INVF, market operator or data reporting services provider, which are appointed in accordance with national law, which are empowered to **set** the entity's **strategy**, **objectives** and **overall direction**, and which **oversee** and **monitor management decision-making** and include persons who effectively **direct** the business of the entity.[19]

**Matched principal trading** - a transaction where the facilitator interposes itself between the buyer and the seller to the transaction in such a way that it is never exposed to market risk throughout the execution of the transaction, with both sides executed simultaneously, and where the transaction is concluded at a price where the facilitator makes no profit or loss, other than a previously disclosed commission, fee or charge for the transaction.

**Multilateral Trading Facility (MTF)** - a multilateral system, operated by an INVF or a market operator, which brings together multiple third-party buying and selling interests in **financial instruments** – in the system and in accordance with non-discretionary rules – in a way that results in a contract.[20] [Inherited from MIFID.] It has been sometimes described as an exchange-lite.

**Organised Trading Facility (OTF)** - a multilateral system which is not a RM or an MTF and in which multiple third-party buying and selling interests in bonds, structured finance products, emission allowances or derivatives are able to interact in the system in a way that results in a contract in accordance with Title II of the MIFIDII directive;[21] [Newly introduced in MIFID II. **Note absence of equities+like**.]

**Systematic internalisers** - INVFs which, on an **organised**, **frequent**, **systematic** and **substantial** basis, **deal on own account** when executing client orders outside a RM, an MTF or an OTF. The **frequent** and **systematic** basis shall be measured by the number of OTC trades in the financial instrument carried out by the INVF on own account when executing client orders. The substantial basis shall be measured either by the size of the OTC trading carried out by the INVF in relation to the total trading of the INVF in a specific financial instrument or by the size of the OTC trading carried out by the INVF in relation to the total trading in the Union in a specific financial instrument. The definition of a systematic internaliser shall apply only where the pre-set limits for a frequent and systematic basis and for a substantial basis are both crossed or where an INVF chooses to opt-in under the systematic internaliser regime; [22]

MIFID I did not define the keywords: **frequent** or **systematic** resulting in a mere 11 firms registering as SIs. MIFIDII does and hence this number is expected to rise following ESMA's publication of EU-wide reference data by 1 August 2018. Further elaboration is provided in delegated regulation of 25-4-2016. For equities[23]:

- On a frequent and systematic basis for **equities** and equity-like, where there is a **liquid market** where during the last **6 months**:
  - o number of OTC transactions carried out by it on own account when executing client orders $>= 0.4\%$ of the total number of transactions in the relevant financial instrument executed in the Union on any trading venue or OTC during the same period

- o the OTC transactions carried out by it on own account when executing client orders in the relevant financial instrument take place **on average on a daily basis.**

- on a frequent and systematic basis for **illiquid** where during the past **6 months** the OTC transactions carried out by it on own account when executing client orders takes place on **average on a daily basis**;

- on a **substantial** basis in the financial instrument where the number of OTC trades carried out by it on own account when executing client orders is, during the past 6 months, >= either:
  - o (i) 15% of the total turnover in that financial instrument executed by the INVF on own account or on behalf of clients and executed on a trading venue or OTC;
  - o (ii) 0.4% of the total turnover in that financial instrument executed in the Union on a trading venue or OTC.

- For SI definitions for bonds, structured finance products, derivatives and emission allowances, refer to Articles 13 - 16 in delegated regulation of 25-4-2016.

- These conditions to be **assessed** on a **quarterly basis** on the basis of **data** from the **past 6 months**. The assessment period shall start on the first working day of the months of January, April, July and October[24].

o For **new INSTRs**: **equity** & equity-like when historical data covers a period of at least 3 **months**. For **bonds**, structured finance products and **derivatives**, **6 weeks**[25].

**Trading Venue** - a Regulated Market (RM), an MTF or an OTF;[26]

# 2
# Timeline

## Recent Timeline

In date descending order:

29 September 2016
FCA published third MIFIDII consultation to seek views on a further set of proposed changes to the FCA Handbook with a focus on investor protection.

29 July 2016
FCA published second consultation entitled: Markets in Financial Instruments Directive II Implementation, to seek views on a further set of proposed changes to the FCA Handbook.

30 June 2016
The Commission adopted a delegated regulation (2016/1033) which contains **limited substantive amendments** to MIFID II and MiFIR, notably regarding the pre-trade transparency for package transactions, the exemption for non-financial entities dealing on own account and the transparency for securities financing transactions.

18 May 2016

The Commission adopted a delegated regulation supplementing MIFIDII. This aims at **specifying**, in particular:

- the rules relating to determining liquidity for equity instruments,

- the rules on the provision of market data on a reasonable commercial basis,

- the rules on publication, order execution and transparency obligations for systematic internalisers,

- and the rules on supervisory measures on product intervention by ESMA, EBA and national authorities, as well as on position management powers by ESMA.


25 April 2016
The Commission adopted a delegated regulation supplementing MIFIDII. The regulation aims at **specifying**, in particular:

- the rules relating to exemptions,

- the organisational requirements for INVFs,

- data reporting services providers,

- conduct of business obligations in the provision of investment services,

- the execution of orders on terms most favourable to the client,

- the handling of client orders,

- the SME growth markets,

- the thresholds above which the position reporting obligations apply and the criteria under which the operations of a trading venue in a host Member State could be considered as of substantial importance for the functioning of the securities markets and the protection of the investors.

7 April 2016

The Commission adopted a delegated directive regarding safeguarding of financial instruments and funds belonging to clients, product governance obligations and the rules applicable to the provision or reception of fees, commissions or any monetary or non-monetary benefits.

3 January 2016

ESMA published and sent to the Commission its second set of Technical Standards (2015/1858) (report date 11-12-2015) 171 pages. This completes the other more substantial report from 28 September 2015.

15 December 2015

FCA published Markets in Financial Instruments Directive II Implementation – Consultation Paper I.

28 September 2015

ESMA published and sent to the Commission its second set of Technical Standards (2015/1464). 402 pages, with an accompanying report

## Key Future Dates

As announced[27] on 30-6-2016 the go-live was postponed by a year, so the new dates are:

- FCA 'will publish a single policy statement covering all aspects of our implementation in 2017[28].' [For UK INVFs, this will be a critical document. Once it has been transposed, it should appear in the FCA's updated handbook which must be carefully scrutinised.]

- 1 February 2017: Trading Venues must have submitted their applications to their National Competent Authorities for **equity** pre-trade transparency waivers.[29]

- 1 Jun 2017: As above but for **bonds and derivatives.**[30]

- 3 July 2017: The transposition of MIFIDII into national laws.

- 1 September 2018: INVFs must have registered as Systematic Internalisers.

- 3 January 2018: The 'date of application' (**go-live**).

Farther afield, the hotly-anticipated **equity consolidated tape** (post-trade transparency – EU-wide consolidated post-trade broadcast) will go live on 3 Sep 2019.[31] The technically challenging non-equity tape will go live later – certainly no earlier than 2020 (ESMA's consultation[32] ended on 5 Dec 2016).

## Brexit

Since 1973, eleven referenda have been held in the UK[33]. On 23 June 2016, the UK voted to leave[34] the EU (Brexit) by a narrow margin of 51.9% to 48.1%.

However, the referendum was merely an expression of will and has no direct legislative impact. The UK currently remains a member of the EU. To leave a Lisbon-treaty 'Article 50'[35] notice must be served by the national government. This triggers the exit negotiations which can last 'two years after the notification'[36]. The UK government appears to be in no rush in triggering the formal process.

Thus, the Brexit has **no** impact on the requirement to implement MIFIDII on affected firms. To quote the FCA[37]:

Much financial regulation currently applicable in the UK derives from EU legislation.

This regulation will remain applicable until any changes are made, which will be a matter for Government and Parliament.

Firms must continue to abide by their obligations under UK law, including those derived from EU law and continue with implementation plans for legislation that is still to come into effect.

Those calling for a *hard-brexit* claim that British financial services companies will be able to circumvent the EU's passporting system (whereby upon receiving authorisation in one member state, they are free to conduct business in the entire Union). This opinion is incorrect. MIFIDII states:

The provision of services by third country firms in the Union is subject to national regimes and requirements. **Firms authorised in accordance with them do not enjoy the freedom to provide services and the right of establishment in Member States other than the one where they are established**...third-country firms should **not** be treated in a more favourable way than Union firms.[38]

In order to continue providing financial services to EU 'eligible counterparties' and 'professional clients', the UK will be obliged to implement MIFID II under equivalence principles, and implement an information-sharing agreement. This is a sensitive topic and, the author suspects, will form centre-stage of the hard-brexit vs. soft-brexit debate. The EU states:

a decision on equivalence...may stipulate whether such decision can be granted in **full or partially, for**

**an indefinite period or with a time limit**. Sometimes, equivalence decisions may apply to the entire framework of a third country or to some of its authorities only. **Some of the equivalence decisions may be subject to specific conditions being satisfied**.[39]

How equivalent the EU Commission deems the UK and what *specific conditions* they choose to impose will be the subject of much negotiation and the long arm of political considerations will be omnipresent during the formulation of these opinions. For retail clients, British firms would be obliged to establish an EU branch which would only be able to provide investment services in the member state where the branch was established.

The House of Commons published an article[40] on 1-August-2016 entitled 'Brexit and financial services' that, while not germane to MIFIDII, provides a useful summary on Brexit.

# 3
# Overview

MIFIR 55 articles

- Regulation establishes uniform requirements in relation to[41]:

- disclosure of trade data to the public;
- reporting of transactions to the competent authorities;
- trading of derivatives on organised venues;
- non-discriminatory access to clearing and non-discriminatory access to trading in benchmarks;
- product intervention powers of competent authorities, ESMA and EBA and powers of ESMA on position management controls and position limits;
- provision of investment services or activities by third-country firms following an applicable equivalence decision by the Commission with or without a branch.
- ESMA has drafted regulatory technical standards to specify the monetary, foreign exchange and financial stability policy operations.

MIFIDII 97 articles

- Definitions
- Member States authorising INVFs.
- Organisational requirements, roles and responsibilities firmed up in Chapter II of (Del. Regulation 25.4.2016, 2016). This includes topics such as General organisational requirements, Compliance, Risk management, Internal audit, Responsibility of senior management, Complaints handling, Remuneration policies and practices, Personal transactions, Outsourcing critical or

important operational functions, Conflicts of interest potentially detrimental to a client.

- Regulated Markets, MTFs, OTFs
- Algorithmic Trading
- Commodity derivatives position limits
- Data Reporting Service Providers
- Competent authorities

Certain articles in both MIFIDII and MIFIR call for ESMA to provide technical details. There are 33 Regulatory Technical Specifications and 11 Implementing Technical Specifications.

When the level I, II and III texts are totalled, there are over 200 MiFID II documents to read.

Further, recall that MIFIDII is a directive which means the details of transposition will come from the member state. This guide has included pertinent technical details with references to the full set.

This book will not delve into obligations on Member States as it is aimed at the investment community.

## Scope: Who does this apply to?

| Principle source: |
| --- |
| 1.      MIFIDII Article 1 |

Applies to **INVFs, market operators, data reporting services providers**, and **third-country firms** providing investment services or performing investment activities through the establishment of a **branch** in the Union.[42]

Also to **credit institutions** when providing specified investment services and/or performing investment activities.[43]

Certain provisions will also apply to **credit institutions** when selling or advising clients in relation to structured deposits.[44]

## Principle exemptions

| Principle sources: |
| --- |
| 1.      MIFIDII Articles 2, 3 <br> 2.      (FCA 3rd Consultation) 1.8 - 1.22 |

- **Insurance** or reinsurance undertakings that are subject to monitoring by the competent prudential-supervision authorities and subject to [the 2009/138/EC Solvency II Directive].[45] The FCA is consulting whether this exemption incorporates 'insurance‑based investment business and pensions.'[46]

- Providing investment services exclusively for their **parent** undertakings, for their **subsidiaries** or for other subsidiaries of their parent undertakings; (as long as they are not MM or have direct access to market or engage in HFT).[47]

- **Incidental** provision of investment service in the course of a professional activity and that activity is regulated by legal or regulatory provisions or a code of ethics governing the profession.[48]

- **Dealing on own account** other than commodity derivatives or emission allowances or derivatives thereof.[49]

- Collective investment undertakings and **pension funds** whether coordinated at Union level or not.[50]

- The [FCA] may exempt certain additional 'Article 3' categories of firms, at their discretion. As of publication date, we await clarification from the FCA.

## Trading Venues (RM, MTF, OTF)

MIFIDII introduces the new concept of an OTF. It 'is broadly defined so that now and in the future it should be able to capture all types of organised execution and arranging of trading which do not correspond to the functionalities or regulatory specifications of existing venues'.[51] Thus, trading venues comprise RMs, MTFs and OTFs.

MTFs resemble exchanges in many ways ('they represent effectively the same organised trading functionality'[52]). They bring together multiple third-party buying and selling interests in financial instruments – in the system and in accordance with **non-discretionary** rules – in a way that results in a contract. Amongst the principle differences is that there is **no listing** facility. The non-discretionary basis is an important feature. By way of example, BATS-Chi-X Europe was an MTF, although it now is a full exchange (RM), authorised for primary listings.[53] Euronext is another example of a RM. TradeWeb is an 'investment firm with permission to operate as a Multilateral Trading Facility ("MTF")'.[54] MTFs are subject to pre and post trade transparency (more on this later), have non-discretionary membership rules and a public rulebook which establishes the operating rules of the MTF. ESMA maintains a list of MTFs in a publicly searchable database.[55]

The **key difference** with between an OTF and MTF is the **discretionary** basis. While RMs and MTFs have non-discretionary rules for the execution of transactions[56] (think of a stock exchange - it cannot choose whether to match your buy order with a sell), the operator of an OTF may carry out order execution on a **discretionary basis** subject to the pre-transparency.

OTF may exercise discretion at two different levels:[57]

1. when deciding to place an order on the OTF or to retract it again and
2. second, when deciding not to match a specific order with the orders available in the system at a given point in time, provided that that complies with specific instructions received from clients and with best execution obligations.

HM Treasury's MiFID II Consultation Impact Assessment (p. 8) noted OTFs are subject to similar organisational requirements to MTFs, however, are distinct from RMs and MTFs in three key ways:

1. the operator of an OTF must play an active role in bringing about transactions on its platform by exercising discretion;
2. an operator of an OTF is subject to conduct rules such as best execution because of the active role they play in bringing about transactions;
3. OTFs are only allowed to trade bonds, certain derivatives, structured finance products and emission allowances, not equity+like.

Hence, OTFs, unlike MTFs[58], are subject to investor protection MIFIDII Articles:

- 24 (general principles and information to clients),
- 25 (assessment of suitability and appropriateness and reporting to clients)
- 27 (obligation to execute orders on terms most favourable to the client), and
- 28 (client order handling rules).

BCG Trader is an example of an OTF. Further salient points:

- OTFs may not deal in equities+like, unlike MTFs and RMs.

- RM[59], MTF[60], OTF[61]: **no execution** of client orders in an OTF **against** the **proprietary** capital. [Note difference with SI.]

- o Exception for OTF only: illiquid sovereign debt instruments.[62]

- RM[63], MTF[64]: not to engage in matched principal trading.

- OTF allowed to engage in matched principal trading in bonds, structured finance products, emission allowances and certain derivatives only where the client has consented to the process. But not derivatives that are subject to the clearing obligation (EMIR). [65]

- OTF cannot be an SI, nor connect with an SI nor connect with another OTF.[66]

# 4

# Trade Transparency, Transaction Reporting & Market Data

*[T]he same pre-trade and post-trade transparency requirements should apply to the different types of venues. The transparency requirements should be calibrated for different types of financial instruments... The requirements should be calibrated for different types of trading, including order-book and quote-driven systems such as request for quote as well as hybrid and voice broking systems...*

*MIFIR[67]*

## PRE-TRADE Transparency

The requirements are split by a) Trading Venue type and b) instrument type (equity + like) and non-equity. I.e. EQ on TV, EQ on SI, non-EQ on TV and non-EQ on SI.

## Equity on Trading Venue

---

Principle sources:

1. MIFIR Articles 3-5
2. RTS 1 (transparency requirements for trading venues and INVFs in respect of shares, depositary receipts, exchange-traded funds, certificates and other similar financial instruments and on transaction execution obligations in respect of certain shares on a trading venue or by a systematic internaliser)
3. https://www.esma.europa.eu/file/19918/download?token=ubOWotD5

---

- **PRE-TRADE** transparency (for equities). **Market operators** and INVFs operating a **trading venue** shall make public (on a **continuous basis** during normal trading hours[68]): current **bid** and **offer** prices, **depth** of trading interests at those prices[69] and **'actionable indication of interest'**.[70]

- The type of information shall be **calibrated for different types of trading systems** including order-book, quote-driven, hybrid and periodic auction trading systems:[71]

*Table 1 Equity Pre-Trade Information to be made Public[72]*

| Type of trading system | Description | Information to be made public |
|---|---|---|
| | A system that by means of an order book and a | The aggregate number of orders and the shares, |

| | | |
|---|---|---|
| Continuous auction order book | trading algorithm operated without human intervention matches sell orders with buy orders on the basis of the best available price on a continuous basis. | depositary receipts, ETFs, certificates and other similar financial instruments that they represent at each price level for at least the five best bid and offer price levels. |
| Quote driven | A system where transactions are concluded on the basis of firm quotes that are continuously made available to participants, which requires the market makers to maintain quotes in a size that balances the needs of members and participants to deal in a commercial size and the risk to which the market maker exposes itself. | The best bid and offer by price of each market maker in shares, depositary receipts, ETFs, certificates and other similar financial instruments traded on the trading system, together with the volumes attaching to those prices. The quotes made public shall be those that represent binding commitments to buy and sell the financial instruments and which indicate the price and volume of financial instruments in which the registered market makers are prepared to buy or sell. In exceptional market conditions, however, indicative or one-way prices may be allowed for a limited time. |
| Periodic auction | A system that matches orders on the basis of a periodic auction and a trading algorithm operated without human intervention. | The price at which the auction trading system would best satisfy its trading algorithm in respect of shares, depositary receipts, ETFs, certificates and other similar financial instruments traded on the trading system and the volume that would potentially be executable at that price by participants in that system. |
| Request for quote | A trading system where a quote or quotes are provided in response to a request for quote submitted by one or more members or | The quotes and the attached volumes from any member or participant which, if accepted, would lead to a transaction under the |

| | | |
|---|---|---|
| | participants. The quote is executable exclusively by the requesting member or participant. The requesting member or participant may conclude a transaction by accepting the quote or quotes provided to it on request. | system's rules. All submitted quotes in response to a request for quote may be published at the same time but not later than when they become executable. |
| Any other trading system | Any other type of trading system, including a hybrid system falling into two or more of the types of trading systems referred to in this table. | Adequate information as to the level of orders or quotes and of trading interest in respect of shares, depositary receipts, ETFs, certificates and other similar financial instruments traded on the trading system; in particular, the five best bid and offer price levels and/or two-way quotes of each market maker in that instrument, if the characteristics of the price discovery mechanism so permit. |

- Orders that are large in scale (**LIS**) [For definition refer to RTS 1, Article 7] or **illiquid** can benefit from a **waiver**[73] from **pre-trade** transparency (i.e. remain dark like a dark pool). The waiver is designed to protect large orders from adverse market impact and to avoid abrupt price movements.

- **Strict criteria for waiver** based on double-**volume cap** requirements:

  o Trading Venue waivers restricted to **4%** of total volume of trading in that instrument on all trading venues across the Union over the previous 12 months.

o    Overall Union trading in a financial instrument carried out under those waivers limited to **8%** of total volume of trading on all trading venues across the Union over the previous 12 months. [74]

My view: will this waiver system work as firms who wish to keep their orders hidden may collate their orders into one large order in order to obtain a waiver? This will likely cause a jump in price when the order is revealed 24 hours later. Further, we know this double-volume cap mechanism was the result of an imperfect compromise that pleased no one. Markus Ferber, a Member of the European Parliament's (MEP's) Economic and Monetary Affairs Committee and rapporteur on the MIFIDII dossier provided rare insight into the MIFIDII formulation of this idea. Ferber noted that the lack of sufficiently accurate data across the Union's markets may render the double-volume cap unworkable or result in it having no impact. It would prove difficult to demonstrate that a particular trading venue in a particular stock has breached either of the percentage caps during any period. The double-volume cap may simply act to direct more trading onto SIs, and therefore result in even less transparency.[75] There will be a review of this mechanism and my prediction is that Ferber's fears will be born out. Only until MIFIDII reporting is timely and of a consistently high quality has this mechanism any chance of succeeding.

Further, there has recently been a slew of announcements by exchanges publicising order matching systems that tout themselves as MIFIDII-compliant mechanisms to circumvent the double-volume cap waiver restriction. Xetra claims its *Volume Discovery Order* system 'allows for MiFID II compliant block trading - without limits, and with maximum execution probability'.[76] Not to be outdone, 'Euronext is introducing a new service that will create more opportunities for market participants to execute large-in-scale orders on its regulated market. The service will enable a major new source of hidden liquidity by leveraging Euronext's Central Order Book…'[77] Bats Europe is 'to Launch New European Equities Large in Scale Negotiation Facility Called Bats LIS'.[78] All systems are in the process of approval and it will be interesting to see the regulator's response.

- Pre-trade transparency market data given access, on **reasonable commercial terms** and on a **non-discriminatory basis**;[79] free[80] after 15 minutes.

## Equity on SIs

| Principle sources: |
| --- |
| 1.　　MIFIR Articles 14,15,17 |
| 2.　　RTS 1 |
| 3.　　(Del. Regulation 18.5.2016, 2016) Articles 12,13 |

Recall from the definitions section that an SI is an INVF which, on an **organised**, **frequent**, **systematic** and **substantial** basis, **deal on own account** when executing client orders outside a RM, MTF or an OTF.[81]

- SI to **make public** firm **quotes** for **liquid** equity + like. For **illiquid**, disclose quotes to their clients upon request[82] for sizes up to standard market size.[83] Obligated to take **all reasonable steps** necessary to ensure that the information to be published is reliable, monitored continuously for errors, and corrected as soon as errors are detected.[84]

- Also time.[85]

- Prices published by SI shall reflect prevailing market conditions where they are close in price, at the time of publication, to quotes of equivalent sizes for the same financial instrument on the most relevant market in terms of liquidity.[86]

- SI **may decide the size** or sizes at which they will quote. The minimum quote size shall be at least the equivalent of 10% of the standard market size [as calculated by competent authority in most liquid market.][87]

- 'Standard market size' for equity + like defined in RTS 1, Article 11

- SI to quote on a regular and **continuous basis** during **normal trading hours**.[88] (Continuous basis - at all times during the hours which the SI has established and published in advance as its normal trading hours.[89]) (Authorities obligated to check regularity of quotes in Article 16.) No obligation during 'exceptional market conditions'[90]. 'Exceptional market conditions' defined.[91]

- SI **access to quotes**: SI decides on the basis of their commercial policy and in an objective **non-discriminatory way**, the clients to whom they give access to their quotes[92]

## Non-Equity on Trading Venue

Principle sources:

1. MIFIR Articles 8-13
2. RTS 2 (regulatory technical standards on transparency requirements for trading venues and INVFs in respect of bonds, structured finance products, emission allowances and derivatives)

**Trading venues** (**Market operators** and **INVF**s) in respect of bonds, structured finance products, emission allowances and derivatives:

- **PRE-TRADE** transparency: make public make public the range of bid and offer prices and the depth of trading interest at those prices[93] calibrated to type of system, below. Notable exemption: derivative transactions of non-financial counterparties which are objectively measurable as reducing risks directly relating to the commercial activity or treasury financing activity of the non-financial counterparty or of that group.[94]

*Table 2 Non-Equity Pre-Trade Information to be made Public*[95]

| Type of trading system | Description | Information to be made public |
|---|---|---|
| Continuous auction order book | A system that by means of an order book and a trading algorithm operated without human intervention matches sell orders with buy orders on the basis of the best available price on a continuous basis. | For each financial instrument, the aggregate number of orders and the volume they represent at each price level, for at least the five best bid and offer price levels. |
| Quote driven | A system where transactions are concluded on the basis of firm quotes that are continuously made available to participants, which requires the market makers to maintain quotes in a size that balances the needs of members and participants to deal in a commercial size and the risk to which the market maker exposes itself. | For each financial instrument, the best bid and offer by price of each market maker in that instrument, together with the volumes attaching to those prices. The quotes made public shall be those that represent binding commitments to buy and sell the financial instruments and which indicate the price and volume of financial instruments in which the registered market makers are prepared to buy or sell. In exceptional market conditions, however, indicative or one-way prices may be allowed for a limited time. |

| | | |
|---|---|---|
| Periodic auction | A system that matches orders on the basis of a periodic auction and a trading algorithm operated without human intervention. | For each financial instrument, the price at which the auction trading system would best satisfy its trading algorithm and the volume that would potentially be executable at that price by participants in that system. |
| Request for quote | A trading system where a quote or quotes are provided in response to a request for a quote submitted by one or more other members or participants. The quote is executable exclusively by the requesting member or market participant. The requesting member or participant may conclude a transaction by accepting the quote | The quotes and the attaching volumes from any member or participant which, if accepted, would lead to a transaction under the system's rules. All submitted quotes in response to a request for quote may be published at the same time but not later than when they become executable. |
| Voice | A trading system where transactions between members are arranged through voice negotiation. | The bids and offers and the attaching volumes from any member or participant which, if accepted, would lead to a transaction under the system's rules |
| Trading system not covered by first 5 rows | A hybrid system falling into two or more of the first five rows or a system where the price determination process is of a different nature than that applicable to the types of system covered by first five rows. | Adequate information as to the level of orders or quotes and of trading interest; in particular, the five best bid and offer price levels and/or two-way quotes of each market maker in the instrument, if the characteristics of the price discovery mechanism so permit. |

- Must make that **information available** to the public on a **continuous basis** during normal trading hours[96]. [My view: cash bonds could prove to be an issue as pre-trade transparency requirements are imposed on instruments on a historical volume basis. Cash bonds are event driven so obligating firms to make bid/offer/depth information on a continuous basis during normal trading could lead to a false market.]

- This must be available to public on '**reasonable commercial terms** and on a **non-discriminatory** basis.'[97] Free after 15 minutes.[98]

- **Waiver available** from PRE-TRADE above transparency for:

  o LIS orders [defined in RTS 2[99]],

  o actionable indications of interest in RFQ and voice trading systems that are above a size specific to the financial instrument, which would expose liquidity providers to undue risk,

  o out of scope derivatives and other illiquid financial instruments.[100]

- Where waiver granted, make public at least **indicative** pre-trade bid and offer prices which are close to the price of the trading interests.[101]

## Non-Equity on SI

> Principle sources:
>
> 1.    MIFIR Article 18
> 2.    RTS 2

- SIs must make public quotes for which they are SIs and for which there is a **liquid** market if:

    o    They receive a RFQ by a client.

    o    They agree. [Note the discretion for non-equities as opposed to the obligation in the case of equities.][102]

- For illiquid non-equities, only obliged if SI agrees.[103]

- SI may update their quotes at any time; only withdraw quote under 'exceptional market conditions'.[104]

- SI allowed to decide, on the basis of their commercial policy and in an objective non-discriminatory way, the clients to whom they give access to their quotes.[105]

## POST-TRADE Transparency

Note in the post-trade transparency space, there is no fundamental different treatment for SIs, albeit they are subjected some extra conditions. Hence, MIFIR buckets them in with trading venues, unlike the pre-trade transparency world. This makes intuitive sense. Once an order has been executed, irrespective of the venue, it should be made public. Consequently, this section is bisected merely into equity + like and non-equity.

## Equity on Trading Venue (and INVF trading outside of Trading Venue), SIs

| Principle sources: |
| --- |
| 1.      MIFIR Articles 6,7,13,20 |
| 2.      RTS 1 Articles 12,14, Annex 1 |

- Make **public the price, volume and time** of the transactions [RTS 1 Annex 1, Table 3 specifies 9 fields] as close to real-time as is technically possible, defined below.[106]

- Where the transaction takes place:
    - **during** the daily **trading hours** of the trading venue, **within 1 minute** of the relevant transaction.
    - **outside** the daily **trading hours** of the trading venue, **before the opening** of the next trading day for that trading venue. [107]

- If executed by SI, must use an APA to make public.[108]

- Access to above on reasonable commercial terms and on a non-discriminatory basis.[109] Free of charge 15 minutes after publication.[110]

- Where a transaction between two INVFs is concluded outside the rules of a trading venue, either on own account or on behalf of clients, only the INVF that sells the financial instrument concerned shall make the transaction public through an APA.[111]

- Deferred publication waiver available for LIS orders.[112]

- **LIS Deferred publication timescales** dependent on Average Daily Turnover of equity and size of transaction, as outlined in RTS 1, Annex 1, Table 4. [The maximum deferral time is by end of the trading day.]

## Non-Equity on Trading Venue (and INV outside of Trading Venue), SIs

| Principle sources: |
| --- |
| 1.  MIFIR Articles 10, 21 |
| 2.  RTS 2 Articles 7-12 |

- Make public the price, volume and time of the transactions executed.[113] [RTS 2 Annex 2, Table 2 specifies 19 fields] As close to real time as possible.[114]

- If executed by SI, must make public by APA.

- 'Real time': for the first three years of application of MIFIR, **within 15 minutes** after the execution of the relevant transaction; thereafter, **within 5 minutes**.[115]

- Deferred publication available for:
  - LIS executions. [RTS 2 Article 13 defines LIS].
  - Illiquid market
  - Above a size that would expose market makers to undue risk.[116]
  - If [FCA] temporarily suspends post-trade reporting for a class due to illiquidity for 3 month periods.[117]

- Deferred publication timescale: make public each transaction no later than 19:00 local time on the second working day after the date of the transaction.[118]

Principle sources:

1.  MIFIR Articles 12-13, 22
2.  (Del. Regulation 18.5.2016, 2016) Articles 7-11
3.  RTS 2 Articles 13-17
4.  RTS 1 Articles 17, 18

- Market operators and INVF operating a trading venue, for all instruments, **PRE** and **POST** trade **data** must be available **separately**.[119]

- Market operators and INVFs operating a trading venue and SIs shall make **market data** available **without** being **bundled** with other services.[120]

- Both PRE and POST data made available on a reasonable commercial basis and non-discriminatory manner. Free after 15 minutes.[121]

- **Reasonable commercial basis**:
  - o  The price of market data shall be based on the **cost** of producing and disseminating such data and may include a **reasonable margin**.
  - o  The cost of producing and disseminating market data may include an appropriate share of joint costs for other services

provided by market operators or INVFs operating a trading venue or by SIs.[122]

- Trading Venue operators and SIs obligated to charge for the use of **market data** according to the use made by the individual end-users of the market data (**'per user basis'**).[123]

- **Prices** for market data shall be charged on the basis of the **level of market data disaggregation**.[124]

- Disclose the price and other terms and conditions for the provision of the market data in a manner which is easily accessible to the public.[125] Next Article 11 contains details of disclosure.

- **Non-discriminatory basis**:
  o make market data available at the same price and on the same terms and conditions to all customers falling within the same category in accordance with published objective criteria.
  o Any differentials in prices charged to different categories of customers shall be proportionate to the value which the market data represents to those customers, taking into account: (a) the scope and scale of the market data including the number of financial instruments covered and their trading volume; (b) the use made by the

customer of the market data, including whether it is used for the customer's own trading activities, for resale or for data aggregation.[126]

Smaller INVFs with little IT infrastructure should consider outsourcing pre and post trade transparency solutions. There are a number of firms offering solutions.[127]

## Consolidated Tape

- NB, Article 65(2) of MIFIDII which mandates CTPs (Consolidated Tape Provider) to publish consolidated data will apply from 3 September of the year **after** go-live.[128] Therefore, CTP go-live is 3 September 2019.

- **CTPs** will consolidate **equity post-trade information** [per RTS 1 Annex 1] into a continuous electronic data stream and made it publicly available real time on a reasonable commercial basis, **free after 15 minutes**.[129]

- **CTPs** will consolidate **non-equity post-trade information** [per RTS 2 Annex 2] into a continuous electronic data stream and made it publicly available real time on a reasonable commercial basis, **free of 15 minutes**.[130] This non-equity obligation will come in force **9 months after** MIFIDII go-live (which is 3 September 2019 for CTPs).[131]

- CTP to ensure data provided is consolidated from all the regulated markets, MTFs, OTFs and APAs.[132]. For **equities**, when a new APA or trading venue comes on line, must incorporate their data within 6 months.[133] - RTS 13 does not specify consolidation information for non-equities due to deferred application (refer to recital 13).

- Published data must be in machine-readable electronic format where computers can connect to it directly in an automated manner.[134]

## Determining liquidity

| Principle source: |
| :--- |
| 1.      (Del. Regulation 18.5.2016, 2016) Articles 1-5 |

- **Share** that is traded daily shall be considered to have a liquid market where[135]:

    o   not less than EUR 100 million for shares admitted to trading on a RM;

    o   not less than EUR 200 million for shares that are only traded on MTFs

    o   Avg no. of transactions $>= 250$

    o   Avg daily turnover $> 1m$ Euros

- Separate criteria for:

51

- Depositary Receipts[136],
- ETFs[137],
- Certificates[138].

• The competent authority of the most relevant market shall assess which of the above have a liquid market and publish results.[139]

# Daily Transaction Reporting

*A transaction report is a data set submitted to us which contains information relating to a transaction. Each transaction report includes information about the financial instrument traded, the firm undertaking the trade, the trade counter party, the person on whose behalf the firm has dealt (where applicable) and the date/time of the trade.*

FCA[140]

*UnaVista Transaction Reporting is an Approved Reporting Mechanism (ARM)…Your data will be validated against the latest data sources to help you spot errors before your reports reach the FCA*

LSE[141]

---

Principle sources:

1. MIFIR Article 26
2. RTS 22 (**DRAFT** technical standards for the reporting of transactions to competent authorities)
3. RTS 22 Annex I, Table 2 (65 fields template for transaction reporting)
4. (ESMA Level III) Transaction Reporting Guidelines
5. FCA 'Transaction Reporting' dedicated page.[142]
6. https://www.handbook.fca.org.uk/handbook/SUP/17/?view=chapter

---

Current state of play: Transaction reporting is currently mandated by MIFID I. The FCA has a Transaction Reporting User Pack (TRUP) 3.1 which outlines INVFs' obligations. Currently, the FCA states that the principle use for this transaction reporting data is to feed into its 'Zen' monitoring system to detect market abuse and market manipulation. The FCA is engaged in a £20 million update of its transaction reporting software. The new system is called MDS. There will be no submission slot required to upload to MDS – it will remain continually open. Users and ARMS will be able to directly query MDS for their own transaction reporting submissions.

Under MIFID II, the volume of data that must be reported is hugely increased from 24 to 65 fields per transaction. Furthermore, the [FCA] will be mandated to utilise the data to calculate instrument liquidity. With the go-live date of January 2018 looming, as of October 2016, RTS 22 remains in draft form. Some firms continue to adopt an ill-advised wait-and-see approach, thereby placing themselves at risk of missing the deadline. Firms should be:

- analysing their financial instrument universe and building out data stores of all in scope instruments,
- liaising with clients to help them obtain LEI identifiers[143],
- building out databases of trader's national ID details and the other personal information mandated in the 65-fields
- building out aggregated position level long/short level information for the short-flag field (explained below).

- ensuring they have reporting agreements with brokers
- deciding on self-reporting vs. ARM reporting for the remainder of transactions.
- For self-reporting, building (or purchasing) solutions to capture an accurate timestamp.

The FCA complains that currently under the less onerous MIFID I requirements, they 'continue to see issues with data quality and completeness'.[144] They have fined many large banks for transactional reporting failures - (e.g. Merrill Lynch £13.2 million[145]). One can only imagine the scenario under MIFID II. It is envisaged that the FCA will initially adopt an accommodating stance while MIFIDII beds in. By Q2 2017, the FCA should have updated its handbook, including Chapter 17 that details transaction reporting obligations. This will constitute the authoritative guide and firms must pour over the text to ensure they are compliant. It will reflect the details in this section.

- INVFs that **execute transactions**[146] must file **post-trade transactions reports** (or an ARM [list of UK ARMS presented in Definitions section] or trading venue acting on its behalf[147]) to the [FCA] as quickly as possible and no later than **COB T+1**.[148] In transaction reporting parlance such an INVF is known as a 'reporting firm.'

- Instruments in scope:

- o financial instruments which are admitted to trading or traded on a trading venue [RM, MTF and OTF]
  - o instruments where the underlying is admitted to trading on a trading venue
  - o instruments where the underlying is an index or a basket composed of financial instruments traded on a trading venue.[149]

Firms are concerned that there is no golden source reference of in-scope reportable instruments, thereby placing considerable burden on them to consider each transaction to assess whether the instrument is subject to the reporting obligation. ESMA *is* obligated to display on its website[150] a comprehensive list of financial instruments that are traded on trading venues or SIs, although ESMA is keen to note this does not represent a golden source.


- Key phrases *transaction* and *executing a transaction* and *order transmission* defined in RTS 22 Articles 2-4. This is a result of confusion and differing interpretations by member states under MIFID I resulting in inconsistency in what triggers a reporting requirement.[151] Broadly,

  - o **Transaction** - the **conclusion** of an **acquisition** or **disposal** of a [MIFIR Article 26(2)] financial instrument.
  - o **Execution of a transaction** - any of: reception and transmission of order,

56

execution of client order, trading on behalf of client, transfer of instruments from accounts

- **Double reporting mitigation.** INVF that intends to transmit the order should agree with the firm receiving the order whether the receiving firm will report all the details of the resulting transaction or transmit the order onwards to another INVF. In the absence of an agreement, the order should be deemed not transmitted and each INVF should submit its own transaction report containing [all] the details that pertain to the transaction that each INVF is reporting.[152]

- **Who must send this report?** By the reporting firm itself, or an ARM acting on its behalf or the trading venue (submitting firms).[153] [E.g. transmitting an order to a broker. If there is a written agreement between a firm and a broker, then the reporting requirement falls with the broker and not the client transmitter. The client would need to send all of the data required for the broker to file the 65-field transaction report. A big decision for INVFs: transmission vs. self-reporting. Does a firm want to send confidential information to brokers?]

- Where transactions have been reported to a trade repository which has been approved as an ARM within same time limit, INVF will have complied.[154]

- **Daily transaction report** to comprise 65 fields,[155] be in electronic and machine-readable form and in a common XML template in accordance with the ISO 20022 methodology.[156] [My view: problematic fields will be the short-selling flag, the LEI identifier and the timestamp. Short sale flag due to requirement to track an aggregated position to establish if one is net long or net short. Further, on a best effort basis an INVF must determine short sales transactions in which its client is the seller, including when an INVF aggregates orders from several clients.[157] [NB cross reference to Client Order Handling chapter for a discussion on order allocation policy.]

- Where a transaction comprises 2 or more instruments, INVF to report each instrument separately, linking the transactions as specified by field 40.[158]

ESMA example:

Where INVF is trading on a Trading Venue for a client on an own account basis it should submit two transactions reports: one for the transaction with the Trading Venue (market side) and the other for the transaction with the client (client side). Where an INVF is acting on a matched principal or 'any other capacity' basis for a single client then it should submit a single transaction report encompassing both the market side and the client side and should include all the fields applicable to the client.[159]

## Reference Data

Principle sources:

1. MIFIR Article 27
2. RTS 23 (data standards and formats for financial instrument reference data and technical measures in relation to arrangements to be made by the European Securities and Markets Authority and competent authorities)

- Trading venues (RMs, MTFs, OTFs) provide [FCA] with reference data for financial instruments. Similarly SIs.[160] Reference data specified in Table 3 of RTS 23, Annex.

- In an electronic and machine-readable form and in a common ISO 20022 XML template.[161]

- By 21:00 CET on each day.[162]

- Prior to admitting a financial instrument for trading, trading venue or SI shall obtain an ISIN.[163]

- Competent authorities [FCA] to transmit complete and accurate data on to ESMA by 23:59 CET same day via the established 'the secure electronic communication channel'.[164]

- ESMA to publish the reference data in an electronic, downloadable and machine readable form.[165]


## Retention of transaction and order Data

| Principle sources: |
| --- |
| 1. MIFIR Article 25 |
| 2. RTS 24 (regulatory technical standards for the maintenance of relevant data relating to orders in financial instruments) |

- **INVFs** shall keep at the disposal of the competent authority, for **5 years**, the relevant **data** relating to **all orders** and **all transactions** in financial instruments which they have carried out, whether on own account or on behalf of a client. In the case of transactions carried out on behalf of clients, the records shall contain all the information and details of the identity of the client, and [other information].[166]

- The operator of a **trading venue** shall keep at the disposal of the competent authority, for at least **5 years**, the relevant data (51-fields[167]) relating to **all orders** in financial instruments. The records shall contain the relevant data that constitute the characteristics of the order, including those that link an order with the executed transaction(s) that stems from that order.[168]

# 5
# Trading & Execution

*It is necessary to establish a comprehensive regulatory regime governing the execution of transactions in financial instruments irrespective of the trading methods used to conclude those transactions so as to ensure a high quality of execution of investor transactions and to uphold the integrity and overall efficiency of the financial system.*

*MIFIDII*[169]

Quick read: Equities to be traded on RM, MTF or SI [not on OTF]. In-scope derivatives subject to the 'trading obligation' must be traded on RM, MTF, OTF and cleared by a CCP. ESMA to publish and maintain exhaustive list of in-scope derivatives classes. OTFs and SIs subject to *best execution* obligations to obtain the *best possible result* for clients. INVFs must publish annual top give execution venues data. Trading Venues must publish quarterly quality of execution data. Clocks to be synchronised to UTC.

# Trading Obligation & Derivatives Clearing (EMIR)

Quick read: MIFIR obligates classes of derivatives (to be decided by ESMA) to be subjected to the *trading obligation (TO)*. These classes of derivatives must be traded on trading venues and cleared by CCPs. There is considerable overlap with EMIR (which establishes *clearing obligations* (COs) for classes of derivatives) although not perfect alignment. This means that there could be certain derivative classes that may be subject to EMIR's CO (listed here[170]), but not MIFIDII's TO. Any differences will eventually iron themselves out as 'under Article 32(1) of MiFIR, every time a class of derivatives (or subset) is declared subject to the CO under EMIR, ESMA has 6 months to prepare, consult on, and present to the Commission a draft RTS stating whether those derivatives should also be made subject to the TO and if so, when.'[171]

| Principle sources: |
| --- |
| 1.     MIFIR Articles 23,28,32 |
| 2.     RTS 4 (criteria for determining whether derivatives subject to the clearing obligation should be subject to the trading obligation) |
| 3.     ESMA Discussion paper (ESMA/2016/1389) |

- INVF obligated to trade shares (admitted to trading on a RM or traded on a trading venue) on a **RM**, **MTF** or **SI**, or an 'equivalent' third-country trading venue. [Note here the **exclusion of OTF**.] Exceptions if trades:

- o are non-systematic, ad-hoc, irregular and infrequent; or

- o are carried out between eligible and/or professional counterparties and do not contribute to the price discovery process.[172]

These **exceptions** should **not be used to circumvent** the overarching obligation: Such an exclusion from that trading obligation should not be used to circumvent the restrictions introduced on the use of the reference price waiver and the negotiated price waiver or to operate a broker-crossing network or other crossing system.[173]

- • Financial counterparties and non-financial counterparties shall **conclude** (non intra-group) **derivative** (that are subject to **the trading obligation**, below) transactions **only on**:

    - o RMs;
    - o MTFs;
    - o OTFs [note inclusion of OTF, unlike equities] or
    - o Third-country equivalent [subject to Commission's equivalency decision] trading venues.[174]
    - o [Note omission of SI, unlike equities.]

- • Derivative classes subjected to *trading obligation* based on two tests[175]:

o   Venue test - the class of derivatives must be admitted to trading or traded on at least one admissible trading venue. Factors include: at least 2 trading market participants; the number of trading venues and the number of market makers.[176]

o   The liquidity test - whether the derivatives are 'sufficiently liquid' and there is sufficient third party buying and selling interest. Factors include: average frequency of trade;[177] average size of trade[178] and average spread.[179]

- **ESMA** shall **publish** and maintain **on** its **website** a register specifying, in an exhaustive and unequivocal manner, the **derivatives** that are subject to the *trading obligation*, the venues where they are admitted to trading or traded, and the dates from which the obligation takes effect.[180]

## Derivatives Clearing

- The operator of a **RM** shall ensure that **all** transactions in **derivatives** that are concluded on that RM are **cleared by** a **CCP** (central counterparty).[181] There are currently 19 CCPs.[182]

- **Indirect clearing** arrangements with regard to exchange-traded derivatives are **permissible** provided that those arrangements **do not increase counterparty risk** and ensure that the assets and positions of the counterparty benefit from protection.[183] The clearing chain must normally be no longer than four chains.[184]

- A **CCP** shall **accept** to clear financial instruments on a **non-discriminatory** and **transparent basis**, including as regards collateral requirements and fees relating to access, regardless of the trading venue on which a transaction is executed.[185] [Refer to RTS 15 for details.]

## Client Order Handling

| Principle sources: |
| --- |
| 1. MIFIDII Articles 28 (+ 20(1)) |
| 2. (Del. Regulation 25.4.2016, 2016) Articles 67-70 |

- INVF to:
    - o ensure that **orders executed** on behalf of clients are promptly and accurately **recorded** and **allocated**;
    - o carry out otherwise comparable client orders **sequentially** and **promptly** (unless the characteristics of the order or prevailing market conditions make this impracticable, or the interests of the client require otherwise);
    - o inform a retail client about any material difficulty relevant to the proper carrying

out of orders promptly upon becoming aware of the difficulty.[186]

- INVF not to misuse information related to pending client orders.[187]

- INVF **may not carry out client order** or a transaction for its own account in **aggregation** with another client order except if 3 conditions are fulfilled:

  o The aggregation is **unlikely** to work to the **disadvantage** any client whose order is being aggregated;
  o it is **disclosed** to each client whose order is to be aggregated that the effect of aggregation may work to its disadvantage in relation to a particular order;
  o an **order allocation policy** is established and effectively implemented, providing for the fair allocation of aggregated orders and transactions, including how the volume and price of orders determines allocations and the treatment of partial executions.[188]

- Where orders are aggregated and only partially executed, allocation will be in accordance with the order allocation policy.[189] Allocation must not be detrimental to client.[190] Client's allocation shall prioritise over the INVF.[191]

- **Client limit order** in respect of shares admitted to trading on a RM or trading venue which are **not immediately executed** under prevailing market conditions, INVFs are, unless the client expressly instructs otherwise, to take measures to facilitate the earliest possible execution of that order by submitting the order for execution to a RM or a MTF or ensuring the order has been published by a data reporting services provider located in one Member State.[192] Member States may decide that INVFs comply with that obligation by transmitting the client limit order to a trading venue.[193]

- OTF operators to prevent the execution of client orders in an OTF against the proprietary capital of the operator of the OTF.[194]

## Best execution

*It is necessary to impose an effective 'best execution' obligation to ensure that investment firms execute client orders on terms that are most favourable to the client.*

*Given that a wider range of execution venues are now available in the Union, it is appropriate to enhance the best execution framework for retail investors.*

*MIFIDII[195]*

Quick read: OTFs and SIs subject to best execution obligations. Must take *all sufficient* steps to obtain the *best possible result* for the client. Total cost including all direct and indirect fees incurred by client a factor. INVF may not receive any remuneration, discount or non-monetary benefit for routing an order to a particular venue. INVF must establish an order execution policy, present it to the client prior to trading and obtain their consent. Upon *material changes*, clients must be notified again for approval. Must be *in sufficient detail and in an easy to understand way*. Executions must be monitored to satisfy compliance. INVF must be able to demonstrate, on request by client, compliance.

---

Principle sources:

1.    MIFIDII Article 27
2.    (Del. Regulation 25.4.2016, 2016) Articles 64-66

---

- INVFs must provide for the prompt, fair and expeditious execution of client orders, relative to other client orders or the trading interests of the INVF.[196]

- **SIs** must **execute** the **orders** they receive from their clients in relation to equity + like for which they are **SIs at** the **quoted prices** at the time of reception of the order **or better**, provided that the price falls within a public range close to market conditions.

- INVFs take **all** *sufficient* **steps** [compare with MIFIDI: all *reasonable* steps] to obtain, when executing orders, the **best possible result** for their clients taking into account:

  o price,
  o costs,
  o speed,
  o likelihood of execution and settlement,
  o size,
  o nature or any other consideration relevant to the execution of the order.

  Nevertheless, where there is a specific instruction from the client the INVF shall execute the order following the specific instruction.[197]

  Note, ESMA has provided further guidance following complaints from INVFs that this was impossible to achieve all the time: 'This overarching requirement should not be interpreted to mean that a firm must obtain the best possible results for its clients on every single occasion.' They expect on-going review of execution arrangements and remedial action if deficiencies are identified.[198]

- **Best possible result.** For **retail clients**: the *total consideration*, representing the **price** and the **costs** relating to execution, which shall include all expenses incurred by the client which are directly relating to the execution of the order, including **execution venue fees, clearing and settlement**

**fees** and any **other fees paid** to third parties involved in the execution of the order.[199]

- INVFs must **monitor** the **effectiveness** of their **order execution** arrangements and execution policy in order to identify and, where appropriate, correct any deficiencies.[200]

- INVFs must be able to **demonstrate** to their **clients**, at their request, that they have **executed** their **orders** in accordance with the INVF's execution policy and to demonstrate to the competent authority, at its request, their compliance [with best executions obligations in Article 27 of MIFIDII][201].

- An INVF shall **not receive any remuneration**, discount or non-monetary benefit **for routing client orders to a particular trading** venue or execution venue which would infringe the requirements on conflicts of interest or inducements set out in paragraph 1 of this Article and Article 16(3) and Articles 23 and 24 of MIFIDII.[202]

- INVFs to establish and implement an **order execution policy**.[203] This policy must be communicated to clients[204]. INVF obtain prior client consent on the order execution policy. INVF must inform client of any material changes.[205] Policy must be reviewed at least annually and when a material change occurs.[206] Details of order execution policy content in Article 66 of (Del. Regulation 25.4.2016, 2016)

- The order execution policy must also **include** a clear and prominent **warning** that any specific **instructions from the client** may prevent the firm from taking the steps needed to obtain the best possible result.[207]

- When executing orders or taking decisions to deal in OTC products including bespoke instruments, INVFs will be required to check the **fairness of the price** that they are proposing to the client, by gathering market data and where possible by comparing against similar products.[208]

  ESMA has provided further guidance: firms should use reference prices where available, utilise [fair] valuation systems, scrutinise inputs and methodologies that underpin valuation models. This is an ex-ante assessment by the firm that takes place prior to the execution of the order.[209]

- INVF who execute client orders must monitor the **effectiveness** of their **order execution** arrangements **and execution policy** in order to identify and, where appropriate, correct any deficiencies. In particular, they shall assess, on a regular basis, whether the execution venues included in the order execution policy provide for the best possible result for the client or whether they need to make changes to their execution arrangements.[210]

- Client **orders** must **not** be **aggregated**, except under strict conditions.[211]

## Quality of Execution Reporting, INVFs

*It is essential to enable the public and investors to evaluate the quality of an investment firm's execution practices and to identify the top five execution venues in terms of trading volumes where investment firms executed client orders in the preceding year.*

*RTS 28[212]*

---

Principle sources:

1. MIFIDII Article 27
2. RTS 28 (the annual publication by investment firms of information on the identity of execution venues and on the quality of execution)

---

- **INVFs** who execute client orders to summarise and **make public** on an **annual basis**, for **each class of financial instruments**, the **top 5 execution venues** in terms of trading volumes where they executed client orders in the preceding year and information on the quality of execution obtained.[213] This must be in a machine-readable electronic format, available for downloading by the public from the firm's website.[214] [My view. This could backfire. Most clients will not analyse the details of top five execution venues in contrast to brokers who will assiduously collate this information from all transmitting INVFs and analyse where INVFs are actually routing their orders as opposed to what they are telling their brokers. This can potentially lead to a recalibration of the INVF-broker relationship based on who is sending more business their way.]

- After excluding SFTs (Securities Financing Transactions)[215], information to include:
    - class of financial instrument;
    - venue name and identifier;
    - volume of client orders executed on that execution venue (as a percentage of total executed volume);
    - number of client orders executed on that execution venue expressed (as a percentage of total executed orders);
    - percentage of the executed orders referred to that were passive (added liquidity[216]) and aggressive (took liquidity[217]) orders;
    - percentage of orders that were directed orders
    - confirmation of whether it has executed an average of less than one trade per business

day in the previous year in that class of financial instruments.[218]

- SFTs to be reported separately according to Table 3 Annex II in RTS 28.

- **INVF** to **publish** for each class of financial instruments, a **summary of the analysis** and conclusions they draw from their detailed monitoring of the quality of execution obtained on the execution venues where they executed all client orders in the previous year. Details of analysis in Article.[219] [My view: demonstrating best execution for OTC may prove problematic. Theoretical fair value prices of OTC products are often discordant with the market; furthermore, they are subjective according to both the valuation model used and the inputs that feed into the model. OTC products are often on a RFQ basis hence short of periodically streaming RFQs it may prove difficult to establish comparison prices.]

## Quality of Execution Reporting, Trading Venues

*With a view to providing both the public and investment firms with relevant data on execution quality to help them determine the best way to execute client orders, it is important to set out the specific content, format and the periodicity of data relating to the quality of execution of financial instruments subject to the trading obligation...*

*RTS 27*[220]

---

Principle sources:

1. MIFIDII Article 27(3)
2. RTS 27 (the data to be published by execution venues on the quality of execution of transactions)

---

- **Scope: trading venues, SIs, MM**s and other **liquidity providers**[221] must **publish** to the public, **without** any **charges**, **data** relating to the **quality of execution** of transactions on that venue on at least an **annual** basis.[222]

- Execution venues to publish **quarterly periodic reports** (no later than three months after the end of each quarter[223]) in a machine-readable electronic format, available for downloading by the public.[224] These will include details about price, costs, speed and likelihood of execution for individual financial instruments (elucidated below).[225]

- Information includes: execution venue name, type, identifier, country; date of the trading day; outages, scheduled actions, failed transactions, value of failed transactions.[226]

- Information on the **type of financial instruments**:
  - name and financial instrument identifier; (or the name and a written description where identifier not available)
  - instrument classification;
  - currency; [227]

- The **price for each trading day** on which orders executed. Intra-day information for trading venues:
  - the simple average price of all transactions that were executed in the two minutes starting at each of the reference times 9.30.00, 11.30.00, 13.30.00 and 15.30.00 UTC on that date and for each size range.
  - SIs, market makers and other liquidity providers : the simple average price of all transactions that were executed in the two minutes starting at each of the reference times 9.30.00, 11.30.00, 13.30.00 and 15.30.00 UTC on that date within size range.
  - Further information per Article 4.[228]

- Details on Costs per Article 5.[229]

- Details on likelihood of execution, per Article 6.[230]

- Further information required for continuous auction order book and continuous quote driven execution venues[231] and RFQ execution venues.[232]

## Reporting Executions to Clients

This section is distinct from post-trade transparency to make public executions via an APA or ARM and T+1 transaction reporting to the [FCA]. The intention here is on obligations to clients.

| Principle sources: |
| --- |
| 1.    MIFIDII Article 25(6) |
| 2.    (Del. Regulation 25.4.2016, 2016) Articles 59-63 |

- Following execution of a transaction on behalf of a client the INVF shall inform the client where the order was executed.[233]

- Confirm execution to client in a durable medium by the next first business day (or if received from third party by next business day following receipt.) Note exception for bonds funding mortgage loan agreements.[234] Confirmation to comprise 16 fields.[235]

- Obligation to update client on status of order on request.[236]

- Details differ for portfolio management per Article 60.

## Clock Synchronisation

Principle sources:

1. MIFIDII Article 50(1)
2. RTS 25 (Level of accuracy of business clocks)

The legislative simplicity of clock synchronisation guises the technical challenges in realising microsecond accuracies. *Hardware* wire timestamps should be considered in preference to software-based solutions. The former tend to be more accurate and reliable; rightly deployed, accuracies into the nanoseconds space can be achieved. Smaller firms will be obliged to seek off-the-shelf solutions due to the technical complexity involved.

- Trading venues and their members or participants **synchronise** the business **clocks** they use to record the date and time of any reportable event[237].

    o Synchronise to UTC[238].
    o Clock sync accuracy defined below:[239]

*Table 1 Level of Accuracy for Trading Venue Operators*

| Trading System gateway-gateway latency | Max. divergence from UTC | Timestamp Granularity |
|---|---|---|
| > 1 millisecond | 1 millisecond | 1 millisecond or better |
| =< 1 millisecond | 100 microsecond | 1 microsecond or better |

*Table 2 Level of Accuracy for members or participants of a Trading Venue*

| Type of trading activity | Description | Max. divergence from UTC | Timestamp Granularity |
|---|---|---|---|
| HFT | | 100 microsecond | 1 microsecond or better |
| Voice trading system | Defined in Article 5(5) of RTS 2 | 1 second | 1 second or better |
| RFQ where the response requires human intervention or where the system does not allow algorithmic trading | Defined in Article 5(4) of RTS 2 | 1 second | 1 second or better |
| Concluding negotiated transactions | MIFIR Article 4(1)(b) | 1 second | 1 second or better |

# 6
# Algorithmic Trading

*...there is the risk of algorithmic trading systems overreacting to other market events which can exacerbate volatility if there is a pre-existing market problem...algorithmic trading or high-frequency algorithmic trading techniques can, like any other form of trading, lend themselves to certain forms of behaviour which is prohibited under [MIFIR]*

*MIFIDII*[240]

Note, for UK INVFs note that *both* the FCA and PRA will be updating their respective handbooks and their respective interpretations may differ slightly. 'This is mostly a result of the two regulators having different objectives; the PRA's proposals focus on the safety and soundness of firms rather than the prevention of market abuse or disorderly markets.'[241] The PRA's rulebook currently has no algorithmic trading section; this will be remedied in their new edition, a draft version is available.[242]

Principle sources:

1. MIFIDII Article 17
2. RTS 6 (the organisational requirements of investment firms engaged in algorithmic trading)
3. Delegated (Del. Regulation 25.4.2016, 2016) Articles 18-20
4. [Interesting FCA paper on dark pool prices: https://www.fca.org.uk/publications/occasional-papers/occasional-paper-no-21-asymmetries-dark-pool-reference-prices ]

**High-frequency algorithmic trading** technique - an algorithmic trading technique characterised by:

(a) infrastructure intended to minimise network and other types of latencies, including at least **1 of the following** facilities for algorithmic order entry: **co-location, proximity hosting** or **high-speed direct electronic access**; [AND]

(b) system-determination of order initiation, generation, routing or execution **without human intervention** for individual trades or orders; AND

(c) **high message intraday rates** which constitute orders, quotes or cancellations;[243]

**High Message Intraday Rate** - average of any of the following: (a) at least 2 messages per second with respect to any single financial instrument traded on a trading venue; (b) at least 4 messages per second with respect to all financial instruments traded on a trading venue.[244]

- Algorithmic trading firm must **notify [FCA]** and **trading venue** of its existence.[245] Note, for UK firms, the PRA is proposing that this notification obligation to the [FCA] suffice and not be extended additionally to the PRA.[246] Note, the FCA will not require third country firms engaged in HFT to notify them.[247]

- INVF must have '**effective systems and risk controls**…to ensure that its trading systems are resilient and have sufficient capacity, are subject to appropriate trading thresholds and limits and prevent the sending of erroneous orders or the systems otherwise functioning in a way that may create or contribute to a disorderly market…'[248]

- Effective systems and risk controls to ensure trading systems do not violate MIFIDII or trading venue rules.[249]

- **Business continuity arrangements**[250] to deal with any disruptive incidents or failure of its trading systems and a timely resumption of algorithmic trading. These to include:

   o a governance framework for the development and of the deployment of the business continuity arrangement;

- o a range of possible adverse scenarios relating to the operation of the algorithmic trading systems;
- o procedures for relocating the trading system to a back-up site;
- o staff training on the operation of the business continuity arrangements;
- o usage policy regarding the *kill functionality;*[251]

- [FCA] may require the INVF to **provide, on a regular or ad-hoc basis,** a **description of** the nature of its **algorithmic trading strategies**, details of the **trading parameters** or limits to which the system is subject, the key compliance and risk controls that it has in place. Trading venue may request this info from [FCA].[252]

- Must **keep records** of above.[253]

- **HFT** INVF must keep **time sequenced records** of all orders including cancellations, executed orders and quotes. Must present to [FCA] upon request.[254] Must **retain** these **records** for 5 years.[255] Details in Annex II of RTS6.

- INVF offering **DEA**: have in place effective systems and controls which ensure a proper assessment and review of the suitability of clients using the service, that clients using the service are prevented from exceeding appropriate pre-set trading and credit thresholds. **INVF responsible to ensure clients** adhere to MIFIDII and trading venue rules.[256] Due diligence assessment on prospective clients obligation.[257] This must be reviewed annually.[258]

- **DEA** must notify [FCA] and trading venue of its presence. [FCA] may request from INVF description of systems and controls and evidence of compliance. Trading venue may request this information from [FCA].[259]

## Market Making

*Two main goals should be attained in specifying the market making obligations of algorithmic traders pursuing market making strategies and the related obligations of trading venues. First, an element of predictability to the apparent liquidity in the order book should be introduced by establishing contractual obligations for investment firms pursuing market making strategies. Second, the presence of those firms in the market should be incentivised, particularly during stressed market conditions.*

*RTS 8[260]*

- **Market making algorithmic** INVF must carry out market making continuously during a specified proportion [half of the trading days over a one month period[261]] of the trading venue's trading hours, except under **exceptional circumstances** [defined in RTS 8[262]]. This must be by binding legal contract with trading venue [content of contract in RTS 8[263]].[264]

- Obligated to: post firm, simultaneous **two-way quotes** of comparable size and competitive prices; deal on their own account in **at least one financial instrument** on one trading venue for **at least 50% of the daily trading hours** of continuous trading at the respective trading venue, excluding opening and closing auctions.[265]

## General Governance

Algorithmic INVF shall **establish:**
- **clear lines of accountability**, including procedures to approve the development, deployment and subsequent updates of trading algorithms and to solve problems identified when monitoring trading algorithms;

- **a separation of tasks and responsibilities** of trading desks on the one hand and supporting functions, including risk control and compliance functions, on the other, to ensure that unauthorised trading activity cannot be concealed.[266]

## Staff

- **Compliance** staff to have at least a **general understanding** of algorithmic trading, and the

INVFs algorithmic trading. Should be in **continuous contact** with people in the INVF who have detailed technical knowledge of the same. Compliance staff should have at all times **contact** with **people in charge of the kill switch**.[267]

- INVF to employ a sufficient number of staff with sufficient technical knowledge of:
  (a) the relevant trading systems and algorithms;
  (b) the monitoring and testing of such systems and algorithms;
  (c) the trading strategies that the INVF deploys through its algorithmic trading systems and trading algorithms;
  (d) the INVF's legal obligations[268]

- INVF to specify above skills. Recruit staff with these skills or train them after recruitment. Ensure they remain up-to-date and evaluate on a regular basis. In particular, staff involved in order submission shall **receive training on order submission systems** and market abuse.[269]

## Testing

- Prior to deployment or substantial upgrade, INVF must **establish development and testing strategy**.[270] These must ensure algorithmic trading strategy: does not behave in an unintended way; complies with MIFIDII, complies with the traded venues rules; does not contribute to disorderly trading conditions; continues to work under stressful market conditions and allows for the switching off of the algorithmic trading system.[271]

- INVF to **adapt** its **testing** methodologies **to the trading venues** and markets where the trading algorithm will be deployed.[272] This and above apply to order execution algorithms.[273]

- Obligation to **keep records of material software changes** related for algorithmic trading:

  o when a change was made;
  o the person who did it;
  o the person who approved it;
  o the nature of the change. [274]

- Obligation to **test conformance** of algorithm **to** the system of the **trading venue** or DMA provider.[275]

- Obligation to have separate test environment from production.[276]

## Deployment & Post-Deployment

- **Before deployment** of a trading algorithm, an INVF shall **set predefined limits** on:
  o (a) the **number** of financial instruments being traded;
  o (b) the **price, value** and **numbers of orders**;

88

- o (c) the strategy positions; and
- o (d) the **number of trading venues** to which orders are sent.[277]

- Obligation to perform **annual self-assessment** and validation and the risk management function[278] to **produce a validation report**.[279] The validation report to be audited by the firm's internal audit.[280]

- Validate the following:
  - o its algorithmic trading systems, trading algorithms and algorithmic trading strategies;
  - o its governance, accountability and approval framework;
  - o its business continuity arrangement;[281]

- Annual self-assessment to include a **stress-test**:
  - o running high messaging volume tests using the highest number of messages received and sent by the INVF during the previous 6 months, multiplied by 2;
  - o running high trade volume tests, using the highest volume of trading reached by the INVF during the previous 6 months, multiplied by 2.[282]

- Requirement for **kill functionality** which cancels immediately, as an emergency measure, any or all of unexecuted orders submitted to any or all trading venues.[283]

- Requirement for **automated surveillance** which effectively monitors orders and transactions, generates alerts and reports and, where appropriate, employs visualisation tools.[284]

## Pre-trade Controls

- Controls:
    - o **Price collars**, which automatically block or cancel orders that do not meet set price parameters.
    - o **maximum order values**, which prevent orders with an uncommonly large order value from entering the order book
    - o **maximum order volumes**, which prevent orders with an uncommonly large order size from entering the order book;
    - o **maximum messages limits**, which prevent sending an excessive number of messages to order books pertaining to the submission, modification or cancellation of an order.
    - o **repeated automated execution throttles** which control the number of times an algorithmic trading strategy has been applied;
    - o set market and credit risk limits;
    - o **automatically block or cancel orders** from a trader if it becomes aware that that

trader **does not have permission** to trade a particular financial instrument. INVF shall automatically block or cancel orders where those orders risk compromising the INVF's own risk thresholds.[285]

## Misc.

- Obligation to implement security measures and limit access to systems. **Annually undertake penetration tests** and vulnerability scans to simulate cyber-attacks.[286]

# 7
# Investor Protection

*Strengthening investor protection is one of the key aims of MiFID II.*

FCA[287]

*The financial crisis highlighted limits in the ability of non-retail clients to fully appreciate investment risks. To address this, MiFID II introduces a number of key changes to the existing client categorisation regime. These include the extension of additional conduct of business requirements to business with Eligible Counterparties (ECPs).*

FCA[288]

Quick read: Key themes: Inducements and research; client categorisation; disclosure requirements regarding the firm, products, costs and charges; client suitability; appropriateness test for complex products; investment advice and independence. Best execution and client order handling are listed under the investor protection section in MIFIDII, but have been included under trading & execution in this tract.

Principle sources:

1. MIFIDII Articles 24-30
2. (Del. Regulation 25.4.2016, 2016) Article 71
3. (FCA 3rd Consultation) Chapter 4

## Client Categorisation

Annex II of MIFIDII details categories of people who are considered professional. They 'possess the experience, knowledge and expertise to make their own investment decisions and properly assess the risks that it incurs'.[289] Thus, they are not afforded the same investor protection provisions as retail clients, unless they actively opt-in. 'They must however be allowed to request non- professional treatment and investment firms may agree to provide a higher level of protection.'[290] Equally, certain category of non-professional (retail) clients may choose to opt-up to be treated as professional clients subject to assessment.[291]

Before engaging in investment activity, an INVF must categorise the client and notify him of this categorisation. The INVFs obligations towards the client differ according to the category.

A number of number of important conduct of business requirements do not apply to eligible counterparties (e.g. the rule on inducements and the obligation to provide best execution).[292]

**Eligible counterparties** - investment firms, credit institutions, insurance companies, UCITS and their management companies, pension funds and their management companies, other financial institutions authorised or regulated under Union law or under the national law of a Member State, national governments and their corresponding offices including public bodies that deal with public debt at national level, central banks and supranational organisations.[293]

- INVF shall **notify** new and existing clients, and existing **clients** of **their categorisation** as a retail client, a professional client or an eligible counterparty.[294]

- INVF shall inform clients in a durable medium about any right that client has to request a different categorisation and about any limitations to the level of client protection that a different categorisation would entail. [295]

- An eligible counterparty may request [an opt-down] to be a treated as an professional or retail client by submitting a written request. Similarly, a professional client may request to be treated as a retail client.[296]

- Elective professional clients will no longer be able to request treatment as an eligible counterparty.[297]

## General

- When providing investment services an INVF must act honestly, fairly and professionally in accordance with the **best interests of its clients**.[298]

- All information, including marketing **communications**, addressed by the INVF to clients or potential clients shall be **fair**, **clear** and **not misleading**. Marketing communications shall be clearly identifiable as such.[299]

- Appropriate information shall be provided in good time to clients or potential clients with regard to the INVF and its services, the financial instruments and **proposed investment strategies**, execution **venues** and **all costs** and related charges.[300]

- **Costs and charges** not associated with market risk to be **aggregated**. Such information provided on a regular basis - at least **annually**. INVF to provide a **breakdown** on request from client.[301]

- When providing **portfolio management** INVF **shall not accept** and retain **fees**, **commissions** or any monetary or non-monetary **benefits** paid or provided by any third. Minor non-monetary benefits that are capable of enhancing the quality of service provided to a client and are of a scale and nature such that they could not be judged to impair compliance with the INVF's duty to act in the best interest of the client are acceptable and shall be clearly **disclosed**.[302]

- An INVF which provides investment services to clients shall ensure that it **does not remunerate** or assess the performance of its staff in a way that **conflicts with its duty** to act in the best interests of its clients. In particular, it shall not make any arrangement by way of remuneration, **sales targets** or otherwise that could provide an incentive to its staff to recommend a particular financial instrument to a retail client when the INVF could offer a different financial instrument which would better meet that client's needs.[303]

- When investment service packaged with others, INVF to inform client whether services are offered separately and if so, the individual costs.[304]

- INVF shall enter into a **written basic agreement** with the client, in paper or another durable medium, with the client setting out the **essential rights and obligations** of the firm and the client.[305]

- INVF shall establish a **record** that includes the document or documents agreed between the INVF and the client that set out **the rights and obligations** of the parties, and the other **terms** on which the INVF will provide services to the client. The rights and duties of the parties to the contract may be incorporated by reference to other documents or legal texts.[306]


## Suitability assessment of client


*When providing investment advice or portfolio management the investment firm shall obtain the necessary information regarding the client's or potential client's knowledge and experience in the investment field relevant to the specific type of product or service, that person's financial situation including his ability to bear losses, and his investment objectives including his risk tolerance…*

*MIFIDII[307]*


*Suitability requirements are intended to ensure that advisers take certain steps when they provide personal recommendations to clients. These steps include getting information on the client's knowledge and experience in relation to the relevant investment field, their financial situation and investment objectives. This is to enable advisers to make a recommendation, or take a decision, which is suitable for that client.*

*FCA[308]*


| Principle sources: |
| --- |
| 1.    MIFIDII Article 25(2) |
| 2.    (Del. Regulation 25.4.2016, 2016) Article 54-58 |
| 3.    (ESMA Level III, Investor Protection) |

- INVF to subject the client or potential client to a **suitability assessment**. INVF to determine the precise extent of information required which should include obtaining details on client's **knowledge** and **experience** [waived for professional clients[309]] in the investment field relevant to the specific type of product or service, their **investment objectives**, tolerance to risk, ability to financially bear losses [assumed able for professional clients[310]] to enable the INVF to assess whether the investment service or product envisaged is appropriate for the client.[311] INVF shall inform clients or potential clients, clearly and simply, that the reason for assessing suitability is to enable the firm to act in the client's best interest.[312]

- The information regarding the **financial situation** of the client or potential client shall include, where relevant, information on the **source** and **extent** of his **regular income**, his **assets**, including **liquid assets**, **investments** and real **property**, and his regular **financial commitments**.[313]

- The information regarding the **investment objectives** of the client or potential client shall include, where relevant, information on the **length of time** for which the client wishes to hold the investment, his preferences regarding **risk taking**, his **risk profile**, and the **purposes** of the investment.[314]

- The information regarding a client's or potential client's **knowledge and experience** in the investment field includes the following, to the extent appropriate to the nature of the client, the nature and extent of the service to be provided and the type of product or transaction envisaged, including their complexity and the risks involved:
  (a) the types of service, transaction and financial instrument with which the client is familiar;
  (b) the nature, volume, and frequency of the client's transactions in financial instruments and the period over which they have been carried out;
  (c) the level of education, and profession or relevant former profession of the client or potential client.[315]

- INVF shall take **reasonable steps** to ensure that the **information** collected about their clients or potential clients is **reliable**.[316] Need to ensure information is up-to-date.

- Where client is two or more people or legal person, INVF must establish, implement and record a policy to decide who is subject to the suitability requirement.[317]

- Where a bundle of services or products is envisaged, the assessment shall consider whether the overall bundled package is appropriate. [similar to investment advice obligation.][318]

- Where INVF assesses a service or product is **inappropriate**, to warn the client. Where information is not forthcoming from client, INVF to warn client they are not in a position advise whether the service or product is appropriate.[319]

- Where INVF only offers execution or reception and transmission of client orders service, at the initiative of the client, no need to obtain prior information, subject to conditions, principle of which is the product must not be complex.[320]

- When providing investment advice, INVF shall provide a **report** to the **retail** client that includes an outline of the advice given and how the recommendation provided is suitable for the retail client, including how it meets the client's objectives and personal circumstances with reference to the investment term required, client's knowledge and experience and client's attitude to risk and capacity for loss.[321]

- Investment firms shall draw clients' attention to and shall include in the **suitability report** information on whether the recommended services or instruments are likely to require the retail client to seek a periodic review of their arrangements. [322]

## Appropriateness

| Principle sources: |
| --- |
| 1.     MIFIDII Article 25(3),(5) |
| 2.     (Del. Regulation 25.4.2016, 2016) Article 56-57 |
| 3.     (FCA 3rd Consultation) Chapter 8 |

An **appropriateness test** is a test by the firm to understand the knowledge and experience of the client. It enables a firm to assess whether a particular **product** or service is appropriate for that client.[323]

The appropriateness test applies to all **complex products**, and products deemed complex cannot be sold execution-only. They are also unlikely to be sold through any direct offer financial promotion, as it is difficult to see how an individual assessment of necessary knowledge and experience of the customer could be undertaken.[324]

- INVF, shall determine [by means of an appropriateness test] whether that client has the necessary experience and knowledge in order to understand the risks involved in relation to the product or investment service offered or demanded. INVF entitled to assume a professional client has the necessary experience and knowledge in order to understand the risks involved in relation to the product or service.[325]

- INVF to retain records of the result of the appropriateness assessments as well as any warnings issues.[326]

## Tied Agents

- Where an INVF decides to appoint a **tied agent,** it remains **fully** and unconditionally **responsible** for any action or omission on the part of the tied agent when acting on behalf of the INVF.[327]

- Tied agents to be registered in **public register**. Must be sufficiently good repute and possess the appropriate general, commercial and professional knowledge and competence.[328]

- INVF only to appoint tied agents from the public register.[329]

- INVF **must keep records** and accounts enabling them at any time and without delay **to distinguish assets held for one client** from assets held for any other client and from their own assets;

  - These records must be accurate and regularly reconciled[330]. [Although refer to next section for potential loophole.]

- Similarly, for financial instruments[331].

- **Funds** must be held in accounts **separate** to the INVF.[332]

- INVF must ensure security interests, liens or rights of set off over client financial instruments or funds enabling a third party to dispose of client's financial instruments or funds in order to recover debts that do not relate to the client.[333]

- Client funds (and financial instruments[334]) may be deposited with third party but (in summary) must be in jurisdiction with broadly equivalent safeguards.[335]

- INVF has no right to use clients financial instrument except with prior written permission.[336]

- INVF must appoint single officer to ensure compliance with regards to safeguarding of client instruments and funds.[337]

## INVF client funds reporting obligations

- INVF shall inform the client or potential client where the financial instruments or funds of that client may be held by a third party on behalf of the INVF.[338]

- INVF shall inform the client or potential client where it is not possible under national law for client financial instruments held with a third party to be separately identifiable from the proprietary financial instruments of that third party or of the INVF from the proprietary financial instruments of that third party or of the INVF and shall provide a prominent warning of the resulting risks.[339] [My view: this point seems to provide an unwelcome loophole that allows the INVF to circumvent (Del. Directive 7.4.2016, 2016) Article 2 (1)]

# 8

# Investment Advice

*[INVF obligated to] disclose the cost of the advice, to clarify the basis of the advice they provide, in particular the range of products they consider in providing personal recommendations to clients, whether they provide investment advice on an independent basis and whether they provide the clients with the periodic assessment of the suitability of the financial instruments recommended to them. It is also appropriate to require investment firms to explain to their clients the reasons for the advice provided to them.*

*MIFIDII[340]*

Quick read: INVF offering investment advice must obtain sufficient prior information about client to understand the essential facts, risk tolerances, ability to bear loss etc. Where information not forthcoming from client, INVF must desist from providing advice. Before advising client to undertake a transaction, INVF shall undertake an analysis of the costs and benefits of the switch, such that they are reasonably able to demonstrate that the benefits of switching are greater than the costs. For retail clients, INVF to provide a report that outlines the advice given and how the recommendation provided is suitable for the retail client, including how it meets the client's objectives and personal circumstances, risk tolerance, capacity to bear loss etc.

INVF must inform client whether advice is independent or not. Advice given exclusively to the public not in-scope. Disclosure to client on whether advice based on broad or restricted analysis of instruments - the type and range of instruments considered, whether a periodic assessment will be provided. Must contain warnings and risks. Disclosure on costs. Costs link to inducements.

Note, the MIFIDII investment advice requirements and their link to the FCA's independent vs. restricted advice categorisation for firms providing advice on retail investment products to retail clients.

---

Principle sources:

1. MIFIDII Articles 24,25
2. (Del. Regulation 25.4.2016, 2016) Articles 52-58
3. (Del. Directive 7.4.2016, 2016) Article 12
4. (FCA 3rd Consultation) 1.25
5. FCA 'Independent and restricted advice' [for firms providing advice on retail investment products to retail clients] webpage

---

**Investment advice** - the provision of **personal recommendations** to a client, either upon its request or at the initiative of the investment firm, in respect of one or more transactions relating to financial instruments.[341]

**Personal recommendation** - a recommendation that is made to a person in his capacity as an investor or potential investor, or in his capacity as an agent for an investor or potential investor. That recommendation shall be presented as suitable for that person, or shall be based on a consideration of the circumstances of that person, and shall constitute a recommendation to take one of the following sets of steps:

(a) to buy, sell, subscribe for, exchange, redeem, hold or underwrite a particular financial instrument;

(b) to exercise or not to exercise any right conferred by a particular financial instrument to buy, sell, subscribe for, exchange, or redeem a financial instrument.[342]


- INVF to obtain from clients and potential clients such information as is necessary for the firm to understand the **essential facts** to have a **reasonable basis** for determining that the transaction recommended:
    - meet the investment objectives of the client in question, including client's **risk tolerance**;
    - client is able to bear related financial risk (loss);
    - client has sufficient knowledge and experience to understand the risks.[343]

- Where INVF does not receive information from client, INVF not to offer advice.[344]

- INVF must inform the client:

    o Whether the advice is provided on an **independent basis or not**;

    o whether the advice is based on a **broad or on a more restricted analysis** of different types of financial instruments and, in particular, whether the range is limited to financial instruments issued or provided by entities having close links with the INVF or any other legal or economic relationships,

    o whether the INVF will provide the client with a **periodic assessment** of the suitability of the financial instruments recommended to that client.[345] [The frequency and extent and where relevant, the conditions that trigger that assessment; the extent to which the information previously collected will be subject to reassessment; and the way in which an updated recommendation will be communicated to the client.[346]]

- Obligation to provide a description of the **types** of financial instruments considered, the **range** of financial instruments and providers analysed per each type of instrument according to the scope of the service, and, when providing independent advice, **how the service provided satisfies the conditions** for the provision of investment advice on an independent basis and the factors taken into consideration in the selection process used by the INVF to recommend financial instruments, such as risks, costs and complexity of the financial instruments.[347]

- Advice must **include** appropriate **guidance** on and **warnings** of the **risks** associated with investments in those instruments or in respect of particular investment strategies and whether the financial instrument is intended for retail or professional clients.[348]

- When offering **advice on transactions**, must collect the necessary information on the client's existing investments and the recommended new investments and shall undertake an analysis of the costs and benefits of the switch, such that they are reasonably able to demonstrate that the benefits of switching are greater than the costs.[349]

- For retail clients, INVF to provide a **report** that includes an **outline of the advice given** and how the recommendation provided is suitable for the retail client, including how it meets the client's objectives and personal circumstances with reference to the investment term required, client's knowledge and experience and client's attitude to risk and capacity for loss.[350]

- Natural persons [**staff**] giving investment advice **possess** the necessary **knowledge and competence**. Member states to publish the criteria used to assess knowledge and competence.[351]

## Independent Basis

- Where an INVF informs the client that investment advice is provided on an independent basis, that INVF shall:

    o assess a sufficient **range of financial instruments** available on the market which must be sufficiently diverse with regard to their type and issuers or product providers to ensure that the client's investment objectives can be suitably met and must **not be limited** to financial instruments issued or provided by: **the INVF** itself or by entities having close links with the INVF; or [linked entities].[352]

Selection process:

- the number and variety of financial instruments considered is proportionate to the scope of investment advice services offered by the independent investment adviser

- the number and variety of financial instruments considered is adequately representative of financial instruments available on the market;

- the quantity of financial instruments issued by the INVF itself or by entities closely linked to the INVF itself is proportionate to the total amount of financial instruments considered; and

- the criteria for selecting the various financial instruments shall include all relevant aspects such as risks, costs and complexity as well as the characteristics of the INVF's clients, and shall ensure that the selection of the instruments that may be recommended is not biased.

    If these 4 points are not fulfilled, the investment advice must not be presented as independent.[353]

- Slightly different conditions for investment advice on an independent basis that **focuses on certain categories** or a specified range of financial instruments.[354]

- For INVFs that offer both independent and non-independent advice:

    ○ In good time before the offering of the advice, in a durable medium inform client which of the two the advice will be.

o   Ensure services and advisors for the two categories are clearly separated so that clients are not likely to be confused as to which category of service they are receiving. A natural person cannot straddle both categories. [355]

## Inducements

- INVF obligated to **rebate to clients** any fees, **commissions** or any monetary benefits paid or provided by any third party or a person acting on behalf of a third party in relation to the services provided to that client as soon as reasonably possible after receipt.[356] Note for UK firms: the FCA proposes to ban advisers receiving inducements in relation to advice on Retail Investment Products (RIPs) even if they intend to rebate them to retail clients.[357]

- INVF to implement a policy for the returning of these monetary benefits. INVF to periodically inform client of monetary benefits transferred to them.[358]

- Minor non-monetary benefits OK but must be clearly disclosed. Further details on 'minor' provided in delegated directive.[359]

# 9
# Research

*…where research is not paid directly by the investment firm out of its own resources but in return for payments from a separate research payment account certain essential conditions should be ensured. The research payment account should only be funded by a specific research charge to the client which should only be based on a research budget set by the investment firm and not linked to the volume and/or value of transactions executed on behalf of clients.*

*Delegated Directive 7.4.2016[360]*

Quick Read: To avoid falling foul of inducement prohibitions, INVF must either directly charge third party from its own funds for research or establish a research payment account. The charge and frequency of charge must be agreed prior to the commencement of an investment relationship. Bundling of research with execution costs, therefore, prohibited. INVF to regularly assess the quality of research. Disclosure of breakdown to client upon request. Financial analysts subject to strict conflict of interest regime including obligation to physically separate analysts from trading and other such functions, separate supervision from other roles and prohibition to engage in trading in researched financial instruments. N.B. a CTP may provide research.[361]

Principle sources:

1.    (Del. Directive 7.4.2016, 2016) Article 13
2.    (Del. Regulation 25.4.2016, 2016) Articles 36-38
3.    RTS 13 Article 13(1)(d)
4.    (FCA 3rd Consultation) Chapter 3

**Investment Research** - research or other information **recommending** or suggesting an **investment strategy**, **explicitly** or **implicitly**, concerning one or several financial instruments or the issuers of financial instruments, including any **opinion** as to the present or future **value** or **price** of such instruments, intended for distribution channels or for the public that is labelled or **described as investment research** or in similar terms. If the recommendation in question were made by an INVF to a client it is not research.[362]

If the above definition is not fulfilled, the material is considered **marketing communication**. There must be a clear statement it is not investment research.[363]

**Financial analyst** - a relevant person who produces the substance of investment research.[364]

- N.B. The FCA is proposing that the MiFID II rules (below) regarding research should apply to firms carrying out collective portfolio management, which includes UCITS management companies and Alternative Investment Fund Managers (AIFMs), but who are not subject to MiFID II.[365]

- To avoid falling fouls of **inducement prohibitions**, provision of **research** by third parties to INVF providing portfolio management or other investment or ancillary services to must be funded either by:

  - o direct payments by the INVF out of its own resources or

  - o payments from a separate **research payment account** controlled by the INVF which has been funded by a **specific research charge** to the client.[366]

## Research Payment Account (RPA)

Where a RPA is established, the following shall apply[367]:

- The RPA is **funded** by a **specific research charge** to the client;

- Note, the FCA is proposing firms can set a shared research budget that applies to *a number* of client portfolios or funds and not on an *individual* client portfolio level.[368] This is because research will often be common to strategies that span multiple clients. Shared budget should not be so broad that portfolios with substantively different research needs are subject to the same budget.[369]

- INVF should document and be able to justify how they have grouped client portfolios for this purpose. Firms must have robust systems and controls to ensure a **fair allocation** of research **costs**.[370]

- The **total amount** of research charges received may **not exceed** the research **budget**.

- INVF to **agree with client** the research **charge** as budgeted by the firm and the **frequency** with which the specific research charge will be deducted from the resources of the client over the year.

- As part of establishing a RPA and agreeing the research charge with their clients, INVFs **set** and **regularly assess** a research **budget** as an internal administrative measure;

- INVF responsible for this account.

- INVF **regularly assesses the quality** of the research purchased based on robust quality criteria and its ability to contribute to better investment decisions.

- INVF obligated to provide client:
  o **before the provision of an investment service** to clients, information about the **budgeted amount for research** and the amount of the estimated research charge for each of them.
  o **annual information on the total costs** that each of them has incurred for third party research.

- Disclosure requirement for INVF upon request by client to provide details of research account.[371]

## Commission Sharing Agreement (CSA)

Much has been made of CSAs and the FCA's desire to ban them by completely unbundling execution commissions from research payments. The FCA stated in its third round consultation, 'MiFID II also allows the firm to collect a client research charge alongside a transaction charge or cost. However, research charges deducted in this way are still required to accrue into a separate RPA.'[372] Also, 'it does not in our [FCA's] view allow brokers providing research to retain charges directly for the research they provide to the investment firm alongside a transaction commission paid by that firm's clients. The research charge must always go to the RPA, and can then be paid out to the relevant broker.'[373]

- Research charges deducted through a broker alongside transaction fees or costs are ceded (or 'swept') to an RPA immediately following the associated transaction (eg daily or within the settlement period for the transaction), although detailed reconciliations may take place less frequently, eg weekly or monthly. [374]

## Conflict of Interest

- INVFs that produce or arrange for the producing of research obliged to ensure financial analysts and others involved in production of research subject to conflict of interest mitigation measures[375]:

  o effective procedures to prevent or **control the exchange of information** between relevant persons engaged in activities involving a risk of a conflict of interest where the exchange of that information may harm the interests of one or more clients;

  o the **separate supervision** of relevant persons whose principal functions involve carrying out activities on behalf of, or providing services to, clients whose interests may conflict, or who otherwise

118

represent different interests that may conflict, including those of the firm;

○ the removal of any direct link between the **remuneration** of relevant persons principally engaged in one activity and the remuneration of, or revenues generated by, different relevant persons principally engaged in another activity, where a conflict of interest may arise in relation to those activities;

○ measures to prevent or limit any person from exercising **inappropriate influence** over [the financial analyst].

○ measures to prevent or control the simultaneous or sequential involvement of a relevant person in separate investment or ancillary services or activities where such involvement may impair the proper management of conflicts of interest.[376]

• Financial analysts and other relevant persons **do not undertake personal transactions** or trade in financial instruments related to the research.[377]

• **Physical separation** (Chinese Wall) between financial analysts and people involved in **trading** in researched instruments. Analysts forbidden from accepting inducements.[378]

- INVF and financial analysts **forbidden** to offer issuers with **favourable coverage**.[379]

- INVF providing **execution** and **research services** as well as carrying out **underwriting** and **placing activities** shall ensure adequate controls are in place to **manage any potential conflicts of interest** between these activities and between their different clients receiving those services.

# 10
# Product Governance

*Product governance refers to the systems and controls firms have in place to design, approve, market and manage products throughout their lifecycle [creation, development, issuance and/or design[380]] to ensure they meet legal and regulatory requirements. Good product governance should result in products that (i) meet the needs of one or more identifiable target markets, (ii) are sold to clients in the target markets by appropriate distribution channels, and (iii) deliver improved consumer outcomes.*

*FCA[381]*

Quick read: MIFIDII places product governance obligations on manufacturers and distributors of financial instruments that are, broadly speaking, the same. Products must go through an approval process before being offered to clients. This applies for *each* financial instrument. A target market must be identified. Those clients for whom the product is inappropriate must also be identified. There will be Board level accountability. There will be compliance oversight. Staff must possess relevant competencies. Product to be subjected to scenario analysis to assess analysis in various market situations. Product must not adversely affect market or harm end client. The charging structure to be analysed to ensure it confirms with objectives of target market. Product to be regularly reviewed. Obligation to pass on information to distributor.

A distribution strategy must be agreed. For the targeted market, obligation to assess whether product meets their identified needs, characteristics and objectives, this includes risk/reward analysis.

Note the repeated use of the phrase *end client*. The manufacturer, thus, is not disposed of liability by offloading the manufactured product onto a distributor.

---

Principle sources:

1. MIFIDII Articles 16(3), 24(2)
2. (Del. Directive 7.4.2016, 2016) Articles 9, 10
3. FCA's The Responsibilities of Providers and Distributors for the Fair Treatment of Customers (RPPD)[382]
4. (FCA 3rd Consultation) Chapter 13

---

- INVF which manufacture financial instruments for sale to clients shall ensure that those financial instruments are designed to meet the needs of an identified target market of end clients within the relevant category of clients, the strategy for distribution of the financial instruments is compatible with the identified target market, and the **INVF takes reasonable steps to ensure that the financial instrument is distributed to the identified target market**.[383]

- INVF which **manufactures** financial instruments for sale to clients shall maintain, operate and review an **approval process** for **each financial instrument** and significant adaptations of existing financial instruments **before it is marketed or distributed** to clients.[384]

- The **product approval process** shall specify an **identified target market** of end clients within the **relevant category** of clients for each financial instrument and shall ensure that all relevant **risks** to such **identified** target market are **assessed** and that the intended **distribution strategy** is consistent with the identified target market.[385]

- Elaboration: manufacturer to **identify** at a sufficiently granular level **the potential target market** for each financial instrument and **specify the type(s) of client** for whose needs, characteristics and objectives the financial instrument is compatible. As part of this process, the firm shall **identify** any **group(s)** of clients for whose needs, characteristics and objectives the financial instrument is **not compatible**. Where INVF manufacturer collaborates only one target market needs to be identified.[386]

- For the targeted market, obligation to assess whether product meets their the identified needs, characteristics and objectives. This is to include an examination of:

    o the financial instrument's risk/reward profile is consistent with the target market; and

    o financial instrument design is driven by features that benefit the client and not by a business model that relies on poor client outcomes to be profitable.[387]

- Manufacturer to consider the **charging structure** for the targeted market to assess compatibility with needs and objectives:

    o financial instrument's costs and charges are compatible with target market;

    o charges do not undermine the financial instrument's return expectations, such as where the costs or charges equal, exceed or remove almost all the expected tax advantages linked to a financial instrument

    o the charging structure of the financial instrument is appropriately transparent and does not disguise costs.[388]

- INVF to **regularly review financial instruments it offers** or markets, taking into account any event that could materially affect the potential risk to the identified target market, to assess at least whether the financial instrument **remains consistent with the needs of the identified target market** and whether the intended distribution strategy remains appropriate.[389] Further, INVF to review prior to any re-issue or re-launch if they are aware of any event that could materially affect the potential risk to investors and at **regular intervals** to assess whether the financial instruments function as intended.[390]

- INVF which manufactures financial instruments shall make available to any **distributor** all **appropriate information** on the financial instrument and the product approval process, including the identified target market of the financial instrument.[391]

- Where INVF offers or recommends financial instruments which it **does not manufacture**, it shall have in place adequate arrangements to **obtain the information** and to understand the characteristics and identified target market of each financial instrument.[392]

- Manufacturer to establish, implement and maintain procedures and measures to ensure the manufacturing of financial instruments complies with the requirements on proper **management of conflicts of interest**, including **remuneration.**

  - manufactured instruments **do not adversely affect end clients** or lead to problems with **market integrity**[393] by enabling the firm to mitigate and/or dispose of its own risks or exposure to the underlying assets of the product, where the manufacturer already holds the underlying assets on own account.[394]

- Obligation to **analyse potential conflicts of interests** each time a financial instrument is manufactured especially where end clients may be adversely affected if they take:

  o an exposure opposite to the one previously held by the firm itself; or

  o an exposure opposite to the one that the firm wants to hold after the sale of the product.[395]

- Manufacturer's relevant **staff** involved in the manufacturing of financial instruments **possess the necessary expertise** to understand the characteristics and risks of the financial instruments they intend to manufacture.[396]

- Manufacturer to ensure that **the management body has effective control** over the firm's product governance process. Ensure that the **compliance reports** to the management body systematically **include information about the manufactured financial instruments**, including **information on the distribution strategy**. INVFs shall make the reports available to [the FCA] on request.[397]

- **Compliance** function **monitors** the **development** and **periodic review** of product governance arrangements in order to detect any risk of failure by the firm to comply with product governance obligations.[398]

- **Written agreement** outlining mutual responsibilities required for INVFs collaborating with non-MIFIDII entities.[399]

- Manufacturers that **distribute** through other INVFs [distributors] shall **determine** the needs and characteristics of clients for whom the product is compatible based on their theoretical knowledge of and past experience with the financial instrument or similar financial instruments, the financial markets and the needs, characteristics and objectives of potential end clients.[400]

  Note here the manufacturer's duty of care is not discharged of by handing the product to a distributor. The manufacturer retains his obligation to assess the characteristic of target clients.

- Manufacturer to **conduct scenario analysis** of their financial instruments which shall **assess the risks of poor outcomes** for end clients posed by the product and in which circumstances these outcomes may occur. Examples of analysis:
  (a) deterioration in the market environment;
  (b) counterparty risks;

(c) the financial instrument fails to become commercially viable; or

(d) demand for the financial instrument is much higher than anticipated, putting a strain on the firm's resources and/or on the market of the underlying instrument.[401]

Distributors have, broadly, the same obligations as manufacturers, per Article 10. [402]

# 11

# Commodity Derivatives

*The communiqué of the G20 finance ministers and central bank governors of 15 April 2011 states that participants on commodity derivatives markets should be subject to appropriate regulation and supervision*

*MIFIDII[403]*

Quick read: NB. The Commission is yet to adopt ESMA's technical specifications related to commodity derivatives, as such the information in this chapter is subject to change. Bloomberg reported[404] that EU parliamentarians have informed the commission in a closed-meeting that they do not feel the curbs on foodstuffs commodity derivatives are strict enough. The Commission wrote[405] to ESMA requesting changes to their draft submission. These include:

- lower minimum limits or a lower baseline for certain agricultural commodities for spot and other months' limits;
- higher maximum limits for illiquid contracts;
- adjustment of the other months' limits where there is a significant discrepancy between open interest and deliverable supply so as to reduce the limits

when the open interest is significantly higher than the deliverable supply and the other way around.

INVFs subject to commodity derivative position limits. INVF to aggregate and net all positions from subsidiaries. Non-financial entities involved in risk reduction measures may apply for an exemption. Baseline limit is 25% of the deliverable supply [ESMA proposing to reduce to 2.5% for liquid contracts with foodstuffs as underlyings and increasing to up to 50% for far out, illiquid months]. Trading venue to make public a weekly report of positions. Trading venue to provide INVF with daily report of its positions. Trading venue and, under exceptional circumstances the competent authority, empowered to oblige INVF to liquidate position, or provide liquidity.

---

Principle sources:

1.    MIFIDII Articles 57,58
2.    (Del. Regulation 25.4.2016, 2016) Article 83
3.    **DRAFT** RTS 20,21

---

- [FCA] to establish and apply **position limits** on the size of a **net** position which a person can hold at all times in **commodity derivatives** traded on trading venues and economically equivalent OTC contracts.

    o    limits set on the basis of all positions held by a person and those held on its behalf at an **aggregate group level**[406]

- Position limits do not apply to positions held by or on behalf of a **non-financial entity** and which are objectively measurable as **reducing risks** directly relating to the commercial activity of that non-financial entity.[407] Such entities shall apply for an exemption to the competent authority for that commodity derivative[408] and shall be notified of its approval or rejection within 21 calendar days.[409]

- Where the same commodity derivative is traded in significant volumes on trading venues in **more than one jurisdiction**, the competent authority of the trading venue where **the largest volume of trading takes place** (the central competent authority) shall set the single position limit to be applied on all trading in that contract.

- [FCA] to determine a baseline figure for the **spot month position limit** in a commodity derivative by calculating 25% of the deliverable supply for that commodity derivative.[410] [ESMA's latest proposal is to reduce this to 2.5% for liquid derivatives with foodstuffs as underlyings.[411]]

- [FCA] to determine a baseline figure for the **other months' position limit** in a commodity derivative by calculating 25% of the open interest in that commodity derivative.[412] [ESMA proposes to widen the range of possible position limits up to 50% for contracts with relatively low levels of liquidity as well as for contracts with few market participants.[413]]

131

## Position Reporting

- Market operator operating a trading venue which trades commodity derivatives or emission allowances or derivatives thereof:

  - make public a **weekly report** with the aggregate positions held by the different categories of persons for the different commodity derivatives or emission allowances or derivatives thereof traded on their trading venue, specifying the number of long and short positions by such categories, changes thereto since the previous report, the percentage of the total open interest represented by each category and the number of persons holding a position in each category. This to be sent to [FCA] and ESMA. **Minimum threshold** for weekly report: 20 open position holders exist in a given contract on a given trading venue; and the absolute amount of the gross long or short volume of total open interest, expressed in the number of lots of the relevant commodity derivative, exceeds a level of four times the deliverable supply in the same commodity derivative, expressed in number of lots.[414]

  - provide the [FCA] with a complete **breakdown of the positions held** by all persons, including the members or participants and the clients thereof, on that trading venue, at least on a daily basis.[415]

- INVF trading commodity derivative or emission allowances outside a trading venue provide the competent authority of the trading venue or the central competent authority where the commodity derivatives or emission allowances or derivatives thereof are traded in significant volumes on trading venues in more than one jurisdiction at least on a daily basis.[416]

- Trading venue to report to INVF its position on daily basis (as well as their clients, all the way till the end client).[417]

## Position Management Powers

- **Trading venue** has powers to[418]:
    - monitor the open interest positions of persons;
    - access information, including all relevant documentation, from persons about the size and purpose of a position or exposure
    - require a person to terminate or reduce a position, on a temporary or permanent basis
    - where appropriate, require a person to provide liquidity back into the market at an

agreed price and volume on a temporary basis.

- The position limits and position management controls shall be transparent and non-discriminatory. Trading venue to inform [FCA] of details of position management controls.[419]

- In exceptional circumstances, competent authority may impose more restrictive position limits for an initial period of 6 months. Details to be published on its website. ESMA to be notified; they are to reply within 24 hours with an opinion regarding whether they consider it justified.[420]

- Competent authorities empowered to impose sanctions for infringements of position limits.[421]

# 12
# Technical Specifications

This chapter is included for ease of reference.

It is important to note that ESMA technical specification documents bear no legal authority in themselves. They merely fulfil ESMA's obligation to present the Commission with technical expertise for the latter to consider and formulate into legislative acts. These are presented to the European Parliament.

Once the Council Of Ministers and the EU Parliament approve, the legislative act will appear in the Official Journal. Only then is it official EU law. Uninformed commentators often fail to understand this nuance.

As matters stand in September 2016, the Commission has adopted most RTSs. For an updated state of play, refer to this document:

http://ec.europa.eu/finance/securities/docs/isd/mifid/its-rts-overview-table_en.pdf

The reader is advised to bookmark it.

# List of RTSs and ITSs

**RTS 1**: Transparency requirements for trading venues and INVFs in respect of shares, depositary receipts, exchange-traded funds, certificates and other similar financial instruments

Annex

**RTS 2**: Transparency requirements for trading venues and INVFs in respect of bonds, structured finance products, emission allowances and derivatives

Annex

**RTS 3**: The volume cap mechanism and the provision of information for the purposes of transparency and other calculations

Annex

**RTS 4**: Criteria for determining whether derivatives subject to the clearing obligation should be subject to the trading obligation

**RTS 5**: Direct, substantial and foreseeable effect of derivative contracts within the Union

**RTS 6**: Specifying the organisational requirements of INVFs engaged in algorithmic trading

Annex

**RTS 7**: Specifying organisational requirements of facilities trading venues allowances and derivatives

**RTS 8**: Market making agreements and market making schemes

**RTS 9**: The ratio of unexecuted orders to transactions

Annex I: Order types

**RTS 10**: Requirements to ensure fair and non-discriminatory co-location services and fee structures

**RTS 11**: Tick size regime for shares, depositary receipts and exchange traded funds

Annex

**RTS 12**: Determination of a material market in terms of liquidity relating to trading halt notifications

**RTS 13**: Authorization, organisational requirements and the publication of transactions for data reporting services providers

**RTS 14**: Specification of the offering of pre-and post-trade data and the level of disaggregation of data

**RTS 15**: Clearing access in respect of trading venues and central counterparties

Annex

**RTS 16**: Access in respect of benchmarks

## REQUIREMENTS APPLYING ON AND TO TRADING VENUES

**RTS 17**: Admission of financial instruments to trading on RMs

**RTS 18**: Suspension and removal of financial instruments from trading reporting service providers

**ITS 19**: Description of the functioning of MTFs and OTFs

Annex: Formats

138

**RTS 20**: [DRAFT] Criteria to establish when an activity is considered to be ancillary to the main business

**RTS 21**: [DRAFT] Application of position limits to commodity derivatives

**RTS 22**: Reporting of transactions to competent authorities

Annex

**RTS 23**: Supply of financial instruments reference data

Annex

**RTS 24**: Maintenance of relevant data relating to orders in financial instruments

Annex

**RTS 25**: Level of accuracy of business clocks

Annex

**RTS 26**: Specifying the obligation to clear derivatives traded on RMs and timing of acceptance for clearing (STP)

139

**RTS 27**: Data to be provided by execution venues on the quality of execution of transactions

Annex I

**RTS 28**: Annual publication by INVF of information on the identity of execution venues and on the quality of execution

Annex

**RTS Authorisation**
**ITS Authorisation** [DRAFT]
**RTS Passporting**
**ITS Passporting** [DRAFT]
**RTS Cooperation between authorities**
**RTS Registration of third country firms**
**RTS**: An exhaustive list of information to be included by proposed acquirers in the notification of a proposed acquisition of a qualifying holding in an INVF [DRAFT]

**ITS**: Standard forms, templates and procedures for the consultation process between relevant competent authorities in relation to the notification of a proposed acquisition of a qualifying holding in an INVF [DRAFT]

# 13
# Resources

## Websites

EU MIFIDII page:
http://ec.europa.eu/finance/securities/isd/mifid2/index_en.htm

FCA MIFIDII page:
https://www.the-fca.org.uk/markets/mifid-ii

FCA Handbook:
https://www.handbook.fca.org.uk/handbook

FCA Transaction Reporting:
https://www.fca.org.uk/markets/transaction-reporting

ESMA MIFIDII page:
https://www.esma.europa.eu/policy-rules/mifid-ii-and-mifir

RTSs:
http://ec.europa.eu/finance/securities/docs/isd/mifid/its-rts-overview-table_en.pdf

Exposing HFT: http://www.nanex.net/NxResearch/

## Key Texts

In date (ascending) order:

- MIFIDII:
  http://eur-lex.europa.eu/legal-content/EN/TXT/?uri=CELEX:32014L0065

- MIFIR:
  http://eur-lex.europa.eu/legal-content/EN/TXT/?uri=CELEX:32014R0600

- **Delegated** Directive of 7-4-2016 regarding to safeguarding of financial instruments and funds belonging to clients, product governance obligations and the rules applicable to the provision or reception of fees, commissions or any monetary or non-monetary benefits.
  http://ec.europa.eu/finance/securities/docs/isd/mifid/160407-delegated-directive_en.pdf

- **ESMA** Report [ESMA/2015/1006] on authorisation, passporting, registration of third country firms and cooperation between competent authorities dated 29-06-2015. [Not discussed in this book]
  https://www.esma.europa.eu/sites/default/files/library/2015/11/2015-esma-1006_-_mifid_ii_final_report_on_mifid_ip_technical_standards.pdf

- **ESMA** Technical Standards [ESMA/2015/1858] dated 11-12-2015 (accepted by Commission on 20-4-2016 on condition certain changes made) https://www.esma.europa.eu/sites/default/files/library/2015-1858_-_final_report_-_draft_implementing_technical_standards_under_mifid_ii.pdf

- **Delegated Regulation** of 25-4-2016 supplementing MIFIDII regarding organisational requirements and operating conditions for INVFs and defined terms. Specifies, in particular, the rules relating to exemptions, the organisational requirements for INVFs, data reporting services providers, conduct of business obligations in the provision of investment services, the execution of orders on terms most favourable to the client, the handling of client orders, the SME growth markets, the thresholds above which the position reporting obligations apply and the criteria under which the operations of a trading venue in a host Member State could be considered as of substantial importance for the functioning of the securities markets and the protection of the investors. http://ec.europa.eu/finance/securities/docs/isd/mifid/160425-delegated-regulation_en.pdf

- **Delegated regulation** of 18-5-2016 supplementing MiFIR. This Regulation aims at specifying, in particular, the rules relating to determining liquidity for equity instruments, the rules on the provision of market data on a reasonable commercial basis, the rules on publication, order execution and transparency obligations for systematic internalisers, and the rules on supervisory measures on product intervention by ESMA, EBA and national authorities, as well as on position management powers by ESMA:

http://ec.europa.eu/finance/securities/docs/isd/mifid/160518-delegated-regulation_en.pdf


- **Delegated regulation** 2016/1033 on 23-6-2016 contains limited substantive amendments to MiFID II and MiFIR, notably regarding the pre-trade transparency for package transactions, the exemption for non-financial entities dealing on own account and the transparency for securities financing transactions. On same date **directive** 2016/1034.

  http://eur-lex.europa.eu/legal-content/EN/TXT/HTML/?uri=CELEX:32016R1033&from=EN

# 14
# Bibliography

CRD VI. (2013). *Capital Requirements Directive 2013/36/EU.*

Del. Directive 7.4.2016. (2016). *EU Del. Directive 7.4.2016.*

Del. Regulation 18.5.2016. (2016). *EU Del. Regulation 18.5.2016.*

Del. Regulation 25.4.2016. (2016). *EU Del. Regulation 25.4.2016.* Delegated Directive.

ESMA Level III. (n.d.). *Transaction Reporting Guidelines.*

ESMA Level III, Investor Protection. (n.d.). Retrieved from https://www.esma.europa.eu/sites/default/files/li brary/2016-1444_mifid_ii_qas_on_investor_protection_topics. pdf

ESMA Technical Spec. 28-09-2015. (2015). ESMA Technical 28-09-2015. Retrieved from https://www.esma.europa.eu/sites/default/files/li brary/2016-1452_guidelines_mifid_ii_transaction_reporting.pd f

FCA 3rd Consultation. (n.d.). *Third Mifid II consultation CP16/29.*

MIFIDII. (2014). *MIFIDII Directive 2014/65/EU.*

MIFIR. (2014). *MIFIR Regulation No 600/2014.*

PRA 1rst Consultation. (n.d.). *First Mifid II Consultation CP/916.*

# 15
# References

[1] http://www.thetradenews.com/Asset-Classes/Fixed-income/Number-of-bond-trading-platforms-available-reaches-128/

[2] https://www.ft.com/content/ba243304-e224-11e6-9645-c9357a75844a

[3] (MIFIR, 2014) Recital (3)

[4] https://europa.eu/european-union/law/legal-acts_en

[5] https://europa.eu/european-union/law/legal-acts_en

[6] Mark Hemsley, chief executive of BATS Chi-X Europe speaking at the Trade Tech Liquidity conference in London on 29.11.2012

[7] (MIFIR, 2014) recital (4)

[8] (MIFIR, 2014) recital (6)

[9] (MIFIR, 2014) recital (8)

[10] (MIFIR, 2014) Article 28(1)

[11] (MIFIR, 2014) Article 1

[12] (MIFIDII, 2014) Article 4(1)(52)

[13] (MIFIDII, 2014) Article 4(1)(54)

[14] https://www.fca.org.uk/markets/transaction-reporting/approved-reporting-mechanisms

[15] (MIFIDII, 2014) Article 4(53)

[16] For further details on the SIP: https://www.ctaplan.com/index

[17] This definition is inherited from EMIR (Article 2(1) of Regulation (EU) No 648/2012), per (MIFIDII, 2014) Article (4) (51)

[18] (MIFIDII, 2014) Article 4(1)(1)

[19] (MIFIDII, 2014) Article 4(1)(36)

[20] (MIFIDII, 2014) Article 4(1)(22)

[21] (MIFIDII, 2014) Article 4(1)(23)

[22] (MIFIDII, 2014) Article 4(1)(20)

[23] (Del. Regulation 25.4.2016, 2016) Article 12

[24] (Del. Regulation 25.4.2016, 2016) Article 17

[25] (Del. Regulation 25.4.2016, 2016) Article 17

[26] (MIFIDII, 2014) Article 4 (24)

[27] http://eur-lex.europa.eu/legal-content/EN/TXT/?uri=OJ%3AL%3A2016%3A175%3ATOC

[28] Markets in Financial Instruments Directive II Implementation: Consultation Paper CP16/19; Point 1.8; https://www.fca.org.uk/publication/consultation/cp16-19.pdf

[29] Answer 3; Page 10; https://www.esma.europa.eu/sites/default/files/library/2016-1424_qa_mifid_ii_on_transparency_topics.pdf

148

30      Answer      3;      Page      10;
https://www.esma.europa.eu/sites/default/files/library/2016-
1424_qa_mifid_ii_on_transparency_topics.pdf

31 (MIFIR, 2014) Article 93

32      https://www.esma.europa.eu/sites/default/files/library/2016-
1425_esma_consults_on_consolidated_tape_for_non-
equity_products_0.pdf

33 http://www.parliament.uk/get-involved/elections/referendums-held-
in-the-uk/

34 http://www.bbc.co.uk/news/politics/eu_referendum/results

35
http://www.europarl.europa.eu/RegData/etudes/BRIE/2016/577971/
EPRS_BRI(2016)577971_EN.pdf

36 Ibid.

37      http://www.fca.org.uk/news/european-union-referendum-result-
statement

38 (MIFIDII, 2014) Recital 109 (emphasis added)

39      http://ec.europa.eu/finance/general-
policy/global/equivalence/index_en.htm

40
http://researchbriefings.parliament.uk/ResearchBriefing/Summary/CB
P-7628

41 (MIFIR, 2014) Article 1 (1)

42 (MIFIDII, 2014) Article 1

43 (MIFIR, 2014) Article 1 (2), MIFIDII Article 3

44 MIFIDII Article 4

45 (MIFIDII, 2014) Article 2

46 (FCA 3rd Consultation) 1.8

47 (MIFIDII, 2014) Article 2

48 (MIFIDII, 2014) Article 2

49 (MIFIDII, 2014) Article 2

50 (MIFIDII, 2014) Article 2

51 (MIFIR, 2014) Recital (8)

52 (MIFIR, 2014) Recital (7)

53 https://www.batstrading.co.uk/about/

54 http://www.tradeweb.com/About-Us/Disclosures/

55
https://registers.esma.europa.eu/publication/searchRegister?core=esma
_registers_mifid_mtf

56 MTF: (MIFIDII, 2014) Article 19 (1)

57 (MIFIDII, 2014) Article 20 (6)

58 (MIFIDII, 2014) Article 19(4)

[59] (MIFIDII, 2014) Article 47 (2)
[60] (MIFIDII, 2014) Article 19 (5)
[61] (MIFIDII, 2014) Article 20 (1)
[62] (MIFIDII, 2014) Article 20 (3)
[63] (MIFIDII, 2014) Article 47 (2)
[64] (MIFIDII, 2014) Article 19 (5)
[65] (MIFIDII, 2014) Article 20 (2)
[66] (MIFIDII, 2014) Article 20 (4)
[67] (MIFIR, 2014) Recital (16)
[68] (MIFIR, 2014) Article 3 (1)
[69] (MIFIR, 2014) Article 3
[70] RTS 1, Article 3(2)
[71] (MIFIR, 2014) Article 3(2) also RTS 1, ANNEX 1, Table 1
[72] RTS1, Annex 1, Table 1
[73] (MIFIR, 2014) Article 4
[74] (MIFIR, 2014) Articles 5
[75] As stated in BestExecution conference held on 4.11.2015 in London
[76] http://www.xetra.com/xetra-en/trading/xetra-release/How-to-trade-large-volume-orders-while-avoiding-market-impact-in-the-future/1973578
[77]

https://www.euronext.com/sites/www.euronext.com/files/if160630ca_new_source_of_liquidity_discovery_to_be_implemented_on_euronext_central_order_book.pdf
[78] http://cdn.batstrading.com/resources/press_releases/Bats-LIS-PR-FINAL.pdf
[79] (MIFIR, 2014) Article 3(3)
[80] (MIFIR, 2014) Article 13
[81] (MIFIDII, 2014) Article (4)(1)(20)
[82] (MIFIR, 2014) Article 14(1)
[83] (MIFIR, 2014) Article 14(2)
[84] RTS1, Article 9
[85] RTS1, Article 9
[86] RTS 1, Article 10
[87] (MIFIR, 2014) Article 14(3)
[88] (MIFIR, 2014) Article 14(1)
[89] (Del. Regulation 18.5.2016, 2016) Article 12
[90] (MIFIR, 2014) Article 15(1)
[91] (Del. Regulation 18.5.2016, 2016) Article 14(1)
[92] (MIFIR, 2014) Article 17(1)
[93] (MIFIR, 2014) Article 8 (1), RTS 2 Article 2
[94] (MIFIR, 2014) Article 8 (1)

95 RTS2, Annex 1
96 (MIFIR, 2014) Article 8 (1)
97 (MIFIR, 2014) Article 8 (3)
98 (MIFIR, 2014) Article 13
99 Defined in RTS 2, Article 13
100 (MIFIR, 2014) Article 9(1)
101 (MIFIR, 2014) Article 8(4)
102 (MIFIR, 2014) Article 18(1)
103 (MIFIR, 2014) Article 18(2)
104 (MIFIR, 2014) Article 18(3)
105 (MIFIR, 2014) Article 18(5)
106 (MIFIR, 2014) Article 6(1)
107 RTS 1 Article 14(1)
108 (MIFIR, 2014) Article 20(1)
109 (MIFIR, 2014) Article 6(1)
110 (MIFIR, 2014) Article 13
111 RTS 1 Article 12(4)
112 (MIFIR, 2014) Article 7(1)
113 (MIFIR, 2014) Article 10
114 (MIFIR, 2014) Article 10
115 RTS 2, Article 7(4)
116 (MIFIR, 2014) Article 11(1)
117 (MIFIR, 2014) Article 11(2)
118 RTS 2, Article 8
119 (MIFIR, 2014) Article 12(1)
120 (Del. Regulation 18.5.2016, 2016) Article 10(1)
121 (MIFIR, 2014) Article 13(1)
122 (Del. Regulation 18.5.2016, 2016) Article 7
123 (Del. Regulation 18.5.2016, 2016) Article 9
124 (Del. Regulation 18.5.2016, 2016) Article 10(2)
125 (Del. Regulation 18.5.2016, 2016) Article 11
126 (Del. Regulation 18.5.2016, 2016) Article 8
127 For example: https://www.tradecho.com (This is not a recommendation to buy)
128 (MIFIDII, 2014) Article 93
129 (MIFIDII, 2014) Article (65)(1)
130 (MIFIDII, 2014) Article (65)(2)
131 RTS 13 Article 21
132 (MIFIDII, 2014) Article (65)(3)
133 RTS 13 Article 15
134 RTS 13 Article 14
135 (Del. Regulation 18.5.2016, 2016) Article 1

[136] (Del. Regulation 18.5.2016, 2016) Article 2

[137] (Del. Regulation 18.5.2016, 2016) Article 3

[138] (Del. Regulation 18.5.2016, 2016) Article 4

[139] (Del. Regulation 18.5.2016, 2016) Article 5(1)

[140] https://www.fca.org.uk/markets/transaction-reporting

[141]     http://www.lseg.com/markets-products-and-services/post-trade-services/unavista/unavista-solutions/mifid-transaction-reporting

[142] https://www.fca.org.uk/markets/transaction-reporting

[143] Some are suggesting obtaining an LEI by paying for the first year's subscription then allowing it to lapse in order to save expensive subscription fees. I do not recommend this.

[144] https://www.fca.org.uk/publication/minutes/transaction-reporting-update-may-14.pdf ; p.13

[145] https://www.fca.org.uk/news/press-releases/fca-fines-merrill-lynch-international-%C2%A3132-million-transaction-reporting

[146] (MIFIR, 2014) Article 26 (1)

[147] (MIFIR, 2014) Article 26 (7)

[148] (MIFIR, 2014) Article 26 (1)

[149] (MIFIR, 2014) Article 26 (2)

[150] (MIFIR, 2014) Articles 27, 34

[151] European Commission, Public consultation: Review of the Markets in Financial Instruments Directive (MiFID), 8/12/2010, chapter 6.2.

[152] RTS 22 Recital (5)

[153] (MIFIR, 2014) Article 26 (7)

[154] (MIFIR, 2014) Article 26 (7)

[155] RTS 22 Table 2 of Annex I

[156] RTS 22 Article 1

[157] RTS 22 Article 11(2)

[158] RTS 22 Article 12

[159] (ESMA Level III) 5.1

[160] (MIFIR, 2014) Article 27 (1)

[161] RTS 23 Article 1

[162] RTS 23 Article 2(1)

[163] RTS 23 Article 3(1)

[164] RTS 23 Article 7(6)

[165] RTS 23 Article 7(1)

[166] (MIFIR, 2014) Article 25 (1)

[167] RTS 24, Annex, Table 2

[168] (MIFIR, 2014) Article 25 (2)

[169] (MIFIDII, 2014) Recital 13

[170] https://www.esma.europa.eu/sites/default/files/library/public_register _for_the_clearing_obligation_under_emir.pdf

[171] Discussion Paper The trading obligation for derivatives under MiFIR; ESMA/2016/1389; Article 4

[172] (MIFIR, 2014) Article 23 (1)

[173] (MIFIR, 2014) Recital 11

[174] (MIFIR, 2014) Article 28 (1)

[175] RTS 4 Recital (1)

[176] RTS 4 Article 4

[177] RTS 4 Article 2

[178] RTS 4 Article 3

[179] RTS 4 Article 5

[180] (MIFIR, 2014) Article 34

[181] (MIFIR, 2014) Article 29 (1)

[182] https://registers.esma.europa.eu/publication/searchRegister?core=esma _registers_mifid_ccp accessed 18.9.2016

[183] (MIFIR, 2014) Article 30 (1)

[184] Indirect clearing relies on a chain of entities performing their respective roles in order to provide access to clearing to the counterparty at the end of the chain. Longer chains are therefore generally more risky.

[185] (MIFIR, 2014) Article 35 (1)

[186] (Del. Regulation 25.4.2016, 2016) Article 67(1)

[187] (Del. Regulation 25.4.2016, 2016) Article 67(2)

[188] (Del. Regulation 25.4.2016, 2016) Article 68(1)

[189] (Del. Regulation 25.4.2016, 2016) Article 68(2)

[190] (Del. Regulation 25.4.2016, 2016) Article 69(1)

[191] (Del. Regulation 25.4.2016, 2016) Article 69(2)

[192] (Del. Regulation 25.4.2016, 2016) Article 70(1)

[193] (MIFIDII, 2014) Article 28 (3)

[194] (MIFIDII, 2014) Article 20 (1)

[195] (MIFIR, 2014) Recitals 91-92

[196] (MIFIDII, 2014) Article 28 (1)

[197] (MIFIDII, 2014) Article 27 (1)

[198] (ESMA Level III, Investor Protection) 1 Best Execution, Question 1

[199] (MIFIDII, 2014) Article 27 (1)

[200] (MIFIDII, 2014) Article 27 (7)

[201] (MIFIDII, 2014) Article 27 (8)

[202] (MIFIDII, 2014) Article 27 (2)

[203] (MIFIDII, 2014) Article 27 (4)

[204] (MIFIDII, 2014) Article 27 (5)

[205] (MIFIDII, 2014) Article 27 (7)
[206] (Del. Regulation 25.4.2016, 2016) Article 66(1)
[207] (FCA 3rd Consultation) 9.27
[208] (Del. Regulation 25.4.2016, 2016) Article 64, (FCA 3rd Consultation) 9.29
[209] (ESMA Level III, Investor Protection) Best Execution Question 2
[210] (MIFIDII, 2014) Article 27(7)
[211] (Del. Regulation 25.4.2016, 2016) Article 68,69
[212] RTS 28 Recital 1
[213] (MIFIDII, 2014) Article 27(6)
[214] RTS 28 Article 4
[215] RTS 28 Article 3(1)
[216] RTS 28 Article 2
[217] RTS 28 Article 2
[218] RTS 28 Article 3(1)
[219] RTS 28 Article 3(3)
[220] RTS 27 Recital 1
[221] RTS 27 Article 1
[222] (MIFIDII, 2014) Article 27(3)
[223] RTS 27 Article 11
[224] RTS 27 Article 10
[225] (MIFIDII, 2014) Article 27(3)
[226] RTS 27 Article 3
[227] RTS 27 Article 3
[228] RTS 27 Article 4
[229] RTS 27 Article 5
[230] RTS 27 Article 6
[231] RTS 27 Article 7
[232] RTS 27 Article 8
[233] (MIFIDII, 2014) Article 27 (3)
[234] (Del. Regulation 25.4.2016, 2016) Article 59(1)
[235] (Del. Regulation 25.4.2016, 2016) Article 59(4)
[236] (Del. Regulation 25.4.2016, 2016) Article 59(2)
[237] (MIFIDII, 2014) Article 50 (1)
[238] RTS 25 Article 1
[239] RTS 25 Annex 1
[240] (MIFIDII, 2014) Recital 62
[241] (PRA 1rst Consultation) Point 4.4
[242] (PRA 1rst Consultation) Appendix 2
[243] (MIFIDII, 2014) Article 4(1)(40)
[244] (Del. Regulation 25.4.2016, 2016) Article 19 (1)
[245] (MIFIDII, 2014) Article 17(2)

[246] (PRA 1rst Consultation) Point 4.7
[247] Private meeting with FCA
[248] (MIFIDII, 2014) Article 17(1)
[249] (MIFIDII, 2014) Article 17(1)
[250] (MIFIDII, 2014) Article 17(1)
[251] RTS 6 Article 14(2)
[252] (MIFIDII, 2014) Article 17(2)
[253] (MIFIDII, 2014) Article 17(2)
[254] (MIFIDII, 2014) Article 17(2)
[255] RTS6 Article 28(3)
[256] (MIFIDII, 2014) Article 17(5)
[257] RTS6 Article 22
[258] RTS6 Article 23
[259] (MIFIDII, 2014) Article 17(5)
[260] RTS 8 Recital 1
[261] RTS 8 Article 1(1)
[262] RTS 8 Articles 3,4
[263] RTS 8 Article 2
[264] (MIFIDII, 2014) Article 17(3)
[265] RTS 8 Article 1(1)
[266] RTS6 Article 1
[267] RTS 6, Article 2
[268] RTS 6 Article 3(1)
[269] RTS 6 Article 3(2),(3)
[270] RTS 6 Article 5(1)
[271] RTS 6 Article 5(4)
[272] RTS 6 Article 5(5)
[273] RTS 6 Article 5(6)
[274] RTS 6 Article 5(7)
[275] RTS 6 Article 6(1)
[276] RTS 6, Article 7
[277] RTS 6, Article 8(1)
[278] RTS 6, Article 9(2)
[279] RTS 6, Article 9(1)
[280] RTS 6, Article 9(3)
[281] RTS 6, Article 9(1)
[282] RTS 6, Article 10
[283] RTS 6, Article 12
[284] RTS 6, Article 13
[285] RTS 6, Article 15
[286] RTS 6, Article 18
[287] (FCA 3rd Consultation)

155

288 (FCA 3rd Consultation) 4.2

289 (MIFIDII, 2014) Annex II

290 (MIFIDII, 2014) Annex II

291 (MIFIDII, 2014) Annex II

292 (FCA 3rd Consultation) 4.27

293 (MIFIDII, 2014) Article 30(2)

294 (Del. Regulation 25.4.2016, 2016) Article 45(1)

295 (Del. Regulation 25.4.2016, 2016) Article 45(2)

296 (MIFIDII, 2014) Article 30(2), (Del. Regulation 25.4.2016, 2016) Article 71(3)

297 (FCA 3rd Consultation) 4.3

298 (MIFIDII, 2014) Article 24(1)

299 (MIFIDII, 2014) Article 24(3)

300 (MIFIDII, 2014) Article 24(4)

301 (MIFIDII, 2014) Article 24(4)

302 (MIFIDII, 2014) Article 24(8)

303 (MIFIDII, 2014) Article 24(10)

304 (MIFIDII, 2014) Article 24(11)

305 (Del. Regulation 25.4.2016, 2016) Article 59(1)

306 (MIFIDII, 2014) Article 25(5)

307 (MIFIDII, 2014) Article 25(2)

308 (FCA 3rd Consultation) 7.1

309 (Del. Regulation 25.4.2016, 2016) Article 54(3)

310 (Del. Regulation 25.4.2016, 2016) Article 54(3)

311 (MIFIDII, 2014) Article 25(2)

312 (Del. Regulation 25.4.2016, 2016) Article 54(1)

313 (Del. Regulation 25.4.2016, 2016) Article 54(4)

314 (Del. Regulation 25.4.2016, 2016) Article 54(5)

315 (Del. Regulation 25.4.2016, 2016) Article 55(1)

316 (Del. Regulation 25.4.2016, 2016) Article 54(7)

317 (Del. Regulation 25.4.2016, 2016) Article 54(6)

318 (MIFIDII, 2014) Article 25(3)

319 (MIFIDII, 2014) Article 25(3)

320 (MIFIDII, 2014) Article 25(4)

321 (Del. Regulation 25.4.2016, 2016) Article 54(12)

322 (Del. Regulation 25.4.2016, 2016) Article 54(12)

323 (FCA 3rd Consultation) 8.2

324 (FCA 3rd Consultation) 8.3

325 (Del. Regulation 25.4.2016, 2016) Article 56(1)

326 (Del. Regulation 25.4.2016, 2016) Article 56(2)

327 (MIFIDII, 2014) Article 29(2)

328 (MIFIDII, 2014) Article 29(3)

[329] (MIFIDII, 2014) Article 29(5)
[330] (Del. Directive 7.4.2016, 2016) Article 2(1)
[331] (Del. Directive 7.4.2016, 2016) Article 2(1)
[332] (Del. Directive 7.4.2016, 2016) Article 2(1)
[333] (Del. Directive 7.4.2016, 2016) Article 2(4)
[334] (Del. Directive 7.4.2016, 2016) Article 3
[335] (Del. Directive 7.4.2016, 2016) Article 2(3-5)
[336] (Del. Directive 7.4.2016, 2016) Article 5(1)
[337] (Del. Directive 7.4.2016, 2016) Article 7
[338] (Del. Regulation 25.4.2016, 2016) Article 49(2)
[339] (Del. Regulation 25.4.2016, 2016) Article 49(3)
[340] (MIFIDII, 2014) Recital 72
[341] (MIFIDII, 2014) Article 4(1)(4)
[342] (Del. Regulation 25.4.2016, 2016) Article 9
[343] (MIFIDII, 2014) Article 25(2), (Del. Regulation 25.4.2016, 2016) Article 54(2)
[344] (Del. Regulation 25.4.2016, 2016) Article 54(8)
[345] (MIFIDII, 2014) Article 24(4)
[346] (Del. Regulation 25.4.2016, 2016) Article 52(5)
[347] (Del. Regulation 25.4.2016, 2016) Article 52(4)
[348] (MIFIDII, 2014) Article 24(4)(b)
[349] (Del. Regulation 25.4.2016, 2016) Article 54(11)
[350] (Del. Regulation 25.4.2016, 2016) Article 54(12)
[351] (MIFIDII, 2014) Article 25(1)
[352] (MIFIDII, 2014) Article 24(7)
[353] (Del. Regulation 25.4.2016, 2016) Article 53(1)
[354] (Del. Regulation 25.4.2016, 2016) Article 53(2)
[355] (Del. Regulation 25.4.2016, 2016) Article 53(3)
[356] (Del. Directive 7.4.2016, 2016) Article 12(1)
[357] (FCA 3rd Consultation) 2.27
[358] (Del. Directive 7.4.2016, 2016) Article 12(1)
[359] (Del. Directive 7.4.2016, 2016) Article 12(3)
[360] (Del. Regulation 25.4.2016, 2016) Recital 27
[361] RTS 13 Article 13(1)(d)
[362] (Del. Regulation 25.4.2016, 2016) Article 36(1)
[363] (Del. Regulation 25.4.2016, 2016) Article 37
[364] (Del. Regulation 25.4.2016, 2016) Article 2(2)
[365] (FCA 3rd Consultation) 1.25
[366] (Del. Directive 7.4.2016, 2016) Article 13(1)
[367] (Del. Directive 7.4.2016, 2016) Article 13
[368] (FCA 3rd Consultation) 3.21
[369] (FCA 3rd Consultation) 3.22

370 (FCA 3rd Consultation) 3.22

371 (Del. Directive 7.4.2016, 2016) Article 13(2)

372 (FCA 3rd Consultation) 3.24

373 (FCA 3rd Consultation) 3.26

374 (FCA 3rd Consultation) 3.24

375 (Del. Regulation 25.4.2016, 2016) Article 37(1)

376 (Del. Regulation 25.4.2016, 2016) Article 34(3)

377 (Del. Regulation 25.4.2016, 2016) Article 37(2)

378 (Del. Regulation 25.4.2016, 2016) Article 37(2)

379 (Del. Regulation 25.4.2016, 2016) Article 37(2)

380 (Del. Directive 7.4.2016, 2016) Article 9(1)

381 https://www.fca.org.uk/publication/minutes/mifid-ii-conduct-forum-minutes-180416.pdf

382 https://www.handbook.fca.org.uk/handbook/document/rppd/RPPD_Full_20160321.pdf

383 (MIFIDII, 2014) Article 24(2)

384 (MIFIDII, 2014) Article 16(3)

385 (MIFIDII, 2014) Article 16(3)

386 (Del. Directive 7.4.2016, 2016) Article 9(9)

387 (Del. Directive 7.4.2016, 2016) Article 9(11)

388 (Del. Directive 7.4.2016, 2016) Article 9(12)

389 (MIFIDII, 2014) Article 16(3)

390 (Del. Directive 7.4.2016, 2016) Article 9(15)

391 (MIFIDII, 2014) Article 16(3)

392 (MIFIDII, 2014) Article 16(3)

393 (Del. Directive 7.4.2016, 2016) Article 9(4)

394 (Del. Directive 7.4.2016, 2016) Article 9(2)

395 (Del. Directive 7.4.2016, 2016) Article 9(3)

396 (Del. Directive 7.4.2016, 2016) Article 9(5)

397 (Del. Directive 7.4.2016, 2016) Article 9(6)

398 (Del. Directive 7.4.2016, 2016) Article 9(7)

399 (Del. Directive 7.4.2016, 2016) Article 9(8)

400 (Del. Directive 7.4.2016, 2016) Article 9(9)

401 (Del. Directive 7.4.2016, 2016) Article 9(10)

402 (Del. Directive 7.4.2016, 2016) Article 10

403 (MIFIDII, 2014) Recital 19

404 http://www.bloomberg.com/news/articles/2016-09-21/commodity-traders-face-tougher-rules-as-eu-fights-market-abuse

405 https://www.esma.europa.eu/sites/default/files/library/2016-668_opinion_on_draft_rts_21.pdf

406 (MIFIDII, 2014) Article 57(1)

[407] (MIFIDII, 2014) Article 57(1)

[408] DRAFT RTS 21 Article 8(1)

[409] DRAFT RTS 21 Article 8(3)

[410] DRAFT RTS 21 Article 9

[411]      https://www.esma.europa.eu/sites/default/files/library/2016-668_opinion_on_draft_rts_21.pdf

[412] DRAFT RTS 21 Article 11(1)

[413]      https://www.esma.europa.eu/sites/default/files/library/2016-668_opinion_on_draft_rts_21.pdf

[414] (Del. Regulation 25.4.2016, 2016) Article 83(1)

[415] (MIFIDII, 2014) Article 58(1)

[416] (MIFIDII, 2014) Article 58(2)

[417] (MIFIDII, 2014) Article 58(3)

[418] (MIFIDII, 2014) Article 57(8)

[419] (MIFIDII, 2014) Article 57(10)

[420] (MIFIDII, 2014) Article 57(13)

[421] (MIFIDII, 2014) Article 57(14)

Printed in Great Britain
by Amazon